To Constance

SWAN FEATHER

With love

Sheona

Portrait of Sheona, 1915

Swan Feather

Recollections in Poetry and Prose

SHEONA LODGE

Where are you bound for with your precious cargo
Lashed in the hold of your wild white swan quill?
Memory's havens impose no embargo –
These you may enter and anchor at will.

FLAMBARD

Published in 1993 by Flambard Press
4 Mitchell Avenue, Jesmond, Newcastle upon Tyne NE2 3LA

Flambard Press wishes to thank Northern Arts for its financial support

Cover design by David Hall
Typeset by Pandon Press Ltd, Newcastle upon Tyne
in association with Janet Starkey
Photographs processed by Tyneside Free Press
Printed in Great Britain by Cromwell Press, Broughton Gifford,
Melksham, Wiltshire

A CIP catalogue record for this book is available from the British Library
ISBN 1 873226 06 3

For
Professor Margaret Macpherson
with love and thanks
for the determination and altruism
wisdom and understanding
with which she nurtured
Swan Feather

ACKNOWLEDGEMENTS

Thank you to everyone who has encouraged me,
especially Elizabeth Brown,.
who mastered the Apple Mac on my behalf,
Jane,
who devoted four days out of a week's holiday
to complete the first draft,
and Juliet Berry and Pamela Mann,
who forged the final link in a chain of coincidences.

S.L.

Some of the material in this book
has previously appeared in the following publications:

Adam's Dream: Poems from Cumbria and Lakeland
(edited by William Scammell and Rodney Pybus, Ambleside 1981)

The American Fly Fisher

Cumbria

The Journal of The Flyfishers' Club

Proceedings of the English Association North
(Volume 5, Liverpool 1990)

CONTENTS

LIST OF ILLUSTRATIONS

INTRODUCTION

The life of Sheona Lodge has nearly spanned the century. Born on 28th January 1901 she has experienced two world wars and, as the wife of a distinguished surgeon, she has seen far-reaching changes in medical practice. Now a great-grandmother, widowed for five years, she lives in Ambleside, enjoying her talent for writing. For her family – daughter Anne, three grandchildren and a great-granddaughter – Sheona continues to form the focal point, and her house, Wraysholme, is something of a United Nations, with friends visiting from all parts of the world.

Sheona was born to Isobel and Herbert Birkinshaw at Ovingham, on the banks of the River Tyne in Northumberland, the second of four children. On her mother's side she was descended from the Hendersons, who were landowners in Northumberland, and on her father's side there were distant connections with the Yeats family in Ireland. Isobel's elder sister Jane and her husband Dr. William Baigent were childless. When Sheona was two years old, her brother had diphtheria and her mother was pregnant, so she was sent to stay with the Baigents at Dunston House, Northallerton, where she was to spend most of her childhood. She remembers saying 'one father, one mother and one little girl is just right'. Thus she adopted the Baigents as 'Mother and Father', while not abandoning her original family, and came to describe herself as 'an only child with two brothers and one sister'.

Fishing was William Baigent's passion. He taught Sheona to tie flies when she was seven or eight and was duly proud when she won First Prize at an Arts and Crafts Exhibition, competing with men – on this occasion he had declined to enter! Jane was probably relieved to pass on her role of fishing companion to Sheona, who in time became a proficient angler in her own right. Her first salmon, a twenty-two-pounder, was the record for the Tees that season. By this time, on condition that she never kept him waiting and read the leading articles and the sports pages of *The Times* daily, Sheona was fit to accompany him to fish the Don. Baigent also provided her with a .22 rifle and a 20-bore gun when she was old enough.

At the age of twelve, Sheona was sent to boarding school at Skellfield, near Ripon. Before that, like many Edwardian children who lived in the country, she had shared a governess with three other children nearby. English was always Sheona's favourite subject at school, although no-one ever told her that she had any ability to write. All the family enjoyed reading and Sheona remembers *A Pilgrim's Progress* being read aloud to her when she was only five years old. While Isobel recited *Hamlet* from memory, William quoted from Tennyson and Gray. Jane provided a more conventional diet of Beatrix Potter, Charles Kingsley and Lewis Carroll.

Sheona saw her brother Frank regularly throughout childhood. After the First World War, during which he went with Lawrence of Arabia on a dangerous mission into the desert, Frank used to accompany Sheona to dances. He had acquired the *Médaille d'Honneur* and claimed to have been kissed by the Empress Eugénie when she presented the medal. Frank studied Medicine and emigrated to New Zealand; one of his daughters is the novelist Fay Weldon.

Bill became a dentist, climbed in the Himalayas and is still able to go up Loughrigg Fell before breakfast. Mary was the first woman in the family to go to university and have a career. Regarded as avantgarde by Jane Baigent because of her socialist principles and her membership of the Fabian Society, Mary became a Peeress in her own right, as Baroness Stewart of Alvechurch. Her husband, Michael Stewart, was Foreign Secretary under Prime Minister Harold Wilson.

When Sheona left school at the age of seventeen, the First World War was nearly over. She helped in the Red Cross hospital and waited anxiously for news of Oliver Lodge, her cousin, who was serving as a surgeon in the Royal Navy. Eight years older than Sheona, he had become her hero.

The end of the War saw the social round established once more and Sheona visited widely among friends and relations. If there was an opportunity to fish she took her rod, and it was while fishing in Scotland that she met Grafton, then an undergraduate at Brasenose College, Oxford. They shared a love of literature, and the friendship developed until eventually Grafton proposed to her at a Commem. Ball beside the lily pond at Worcester College. Sheona havered. She was far from decided. Grafton refused to accept rejection. Life, which up to now had been comparatively light-hearted, became complex and difficult. She was trying hard not to fall in love with her cousin Oliver, but after a skiing holiday in Switzerland with a group of friends including Oliver her mind was made up. She and Oliver were married on 24th June 1924.

The next thirty-five years were spent in the West Riding of Yorkshire. Oliver was an eye, ear, nose and throat surgeon whose main hospital bases were Bradford, Halifax and Huddersfield, cities blackened by smoke from the mill chimneys. He was also a pioneer in brain surgery. In 1934 he was the first to plant radon seeds in tumours of the pituitary gland. They lived in Halifax and, as the wife of a busy surgeon, Sheona had little time to spare. In the years between

the wars without antibiotics, brain abscesses, mastoiditis and diph-
theria were potentially fatal. There were frequent night calls to fever
hospitals where children needed life-saving tracheotomies. When
Oliver returned, Sheona was up to refill the hot water bottle, provide
a disinfectant bath and a hot milky drink.

The Lodges had two children; Anne, born in 1925, and Fiona who
was born ten years later. Fiona was delicate from birth. Sheona was
told 'you will never raise that child' but they did. She died of leu-
kaemia in 1980. Anne continued the family medical tradition by qual-
ifying as a doctor and specialising in psychotherapy; her daughter
Jane is now a doctor working with *Médecins du Monde*.

After the Second World War and the establishment of the National
Health Service in 1948, Oliver specialised in E.N.T. surgery and gave
up work on eyes. He was a founder Fellow of the International Col-
lege of Surgeons, and was invited as guest speaker to conferences
throughout the world. Sheona, sometimes joined by Anne, accompa-
nied him on these visits.

In 1959 they retired to the house, Wraysholme, that Fiona found in
Ambleside, set in an acre of tranquil garden overlooking Loughrigg
Fell. Oliver became engrossed in painting and playing the organ in a
local church, and Sheona found sufficient confidence to respond to a
request from the Editor of *The Journal of The Flyfishers' Club* to provide
a memoir of William Baigent. Recollections of fishing expeditions
with Father provided Sheona with her first published pieces of writ-
ing, and for over twenty years she has been a regular contributor of
poems and prose articles to that journal and, to a lesser extent, *The
American Fly Fisher*.

In 1987 Oliver's energy began to fade and he died on New Year's
Eve with Sheona holding his hand. That afternoon, they had sat
together watching *Kim* on television, waiting for the Lama to find
The River. Oliver was ninety-three years old.

As Sheona came to terms with Oliver's death, thinking back over
her early life and their years together, she began to write short pieces
of prose and poems to capture particular moments of time. Her mem-
ories, flowing freely like one of the northern rivers that she knew so
well, have their pools, rivulets, and strong, surging currents. These
recollections have the delicacy of the swan's feather in the stream,
but also its resilience and strength. *Swan Feather* is full of unexpected
delights. It is a unique achievement.

THE EDITORS
May 1993

Jane Baigent (née Garbutt)

Two Sisters

Isobel Birkinshaw (née Garbutt)

PREFACE
JIGSAW TO SWAN FEATHER

*Days when summers were hot, flowers smelled sweet and jigsaw pieces
were made of wood instead of cardboard, and slipped smoothly into place.
There were boxes of jigsaws in the bottom of Mother's bureau; on the lids
were pictures of cottage gardens and hunting scenes.*

When I look at the lid of my jigsaw I see a river.

*We searched for the sources of rivers, Father and I. We marvelled when
we came to a watershed. Father told me of the salmon's journey from mid-
Atlantic to his natal river. At the same time 'The Water Babies' and 'A Pil-
grim's Progress' were being read to me. The three still seem inextricably
entwined.*

*First the salmon surmounting seemingly unscalable falls. Then Tom, the
Water Baby, his stream like the Beck, and the bells he heard could have been
our curfew that tolled every night at eight. Christian's river was deep and
there was no bridge. The Swale where we fished had been blessed by Pauli-
nus and he'd baptised 'above ten thousand men, beside an innumerable
multitude of women and children'.*

*Journeys by road or by waterway held hazards and miracles and required
courage. Jigsaw pieces are hard and tend to become lost. Memories weigh
nothing, would easily fit into the hold of a swan quill.*

*St. Anthony, who can never have known a jigsaw, must have seen many
a swan quill or feather float past him as he preached to the fishes.*

Sheona talking to the computer
(Photo: Paul Renouf)

Chapter One

TALKING TO THE COMPUTER

How it began

Oliver was ninety-three, he had been in hospital for two months; he had lost the urge to paint, to write poetry, to play bridge or the organ. Anne thought that he should have an interest to occupy his active mind – she bought him this Amstrad. He lay in bed looking at it sadly. There was no alternative, I had to learn how to cope with the creature.

Owning a computer is akin to marriage with a foreigner: not only does one become a partner rather than an individual, one has to learn a new language. Amstrad had only one direction that made sense to me: it said 'Create a File'. This was my first attempt. I began with a quotation from a favourite poem, 'Ulysses' by Alfred, Lord Tennyson.

ODE TO O

'To sail beyond the sunset and the baths
Of all the western stars,' only on land
And in an open Morris with your hand
In mine, not daring to believe our paths
Could lead along 'untrodden ways' despite
Hazards seeming insuperable then.
That day you tailed my salmon – a clean ten-
Pounder – in the Cauldron Pool. Now the light
Begins to fade. 'Time out of Mind' they say,
Yet how it floods my memory that hour
(I was just seventeen, you twenty-four)
As sadly I put rod, reel, gaff away.
Begone with sentiment! Without ado.
Come new computer, print an ode to you.

Oliver's outward reaction to this was to wonder if Amstrad could keep accounts. I tried a simple sum. 'Three and three and three' I asked, 'Seventeen' came the answer. I rang Paul at the computer shop. 'You've got the formula wrong,' he said. We decided to keep to Word Processing. Incidentally, the Ode is not an ode, but a not very good sonnet.

Oliver died on New Year's Eve, 1987. Sorrow is like a river in flood: however hard one tries to bolster its banks, some time it breaks through. We can't help being part of the river; maybe we hope that bits and pieces – flotsam and jetsam – will gather in some backwater and be discovered in time.

Flotsam

Flotsam for me happened to be the contents of Oliver's filing cabinet: I had not expected it to contain documents of importance, the key had long been lost. It took the ingenuity of a designer of submarines to open it; it would have delighted Oliver to watch fingers sensitive as his own manipulating each spring.

First I discovered his commission in the Royal Army Medical Corps; I knew the story. In August 1914, entering his final year as a medical student, Oliver was in camp on Salisbury Plain with the Officers' Training Corps. General French told them that the cavalry was outdated and would hardly play a role in the coming war.

By the time Oliver's commission for the R.A.M.C. arrived, he was already a Surgeon Probationer in *H.M.S. Ghurka*, shortly to bring the first German U-boat to the surface with its crew alive – 'very decent fellows,' said Oliver. His photograph of the capture found its way to the front page of the *Daily Mail*. He was given a cheque for £100, which he donated to the Mine Sweepers' Fund. Its patroness, Princess Louis of Battenberg, wrote a letter of thanks and invited him to an 'At Home'; other duties intervened!

I also found an account of the Kitchener story in Oliver's files. The *Ghurka* was ordered to take an 'important personage' to France. There was no concealing his identity, his picture was on every poster pointing a finger and saying 'Your King and Country Need You'. These are Oliver's words (his war letters are in the Imperial War Museum):

> The wind would be about force 9. The ship's company was fully occupied, training the torpedo tubes outboard and making everything secure; consequently it fell upon me to receive him. This was during the darkest days of the Western Front, so it was not surprising that he stood like Napoleon on board the *Bellerephon* in sombre meditation. I felt it my duty to inform his A.D.C., Col. Seeley, that the moment we left the shelter of the Western Entrance at Dover and altered course for our destination, the quarter deck would be washed down by waves and

would be unsafe. Eventually I managed to convince the reluctant General himself and led the pair forward to the Captain's cabin on the fore bridge.

Then, being coding officer, I went below to prepare the signal to be flashed to Gris Nez, before entering the harbour at Boulogne. The code, 'identification and request for permission to enter', an elaborate one, had to be corrected periodically. From Gris Nez there was no response and I was assured that if I was at fault I would be court martialled. Finally the search light was switched on and we entered the harbour.

The next day, the Harbour Master declined to come on board, explaining to our emissary that, as the international codes were weighted with lead and labelled 'To be thrown overboard in the event of imminent capture by the enemy' and were consigned to a safe, next time would we kindly sound our siren three times as usual.

*1988: Anne read this, 'No-one is interested in Kitchener,' thus dismissing the man we thought had come to win the war. 'Tell me about **your** war,' she said.*

School

War years were school years for me. There were some new girls from Belgium. We were allowed to speak to them only in English. In *The Times* we read of atrocities committed by Germans in their country. Other Belgian refugees found shelter in the County Hall, Northallerton, half of which had become a Red Cross Hospital. Father was Commandant and Medical Officer.

My schoolfriend Marjorie's father, a Colonel in the Central India Horse, was coming home to fight in France. She taught me to sing 'It's a Long Way to Tipperary' in Hindustani. Together, we read Kipling's *Barrack Room Ballads* and *Soldiers Three*. Marjorie had letters from the Editor of *The Times*, Geoffrey Dawson, a family friend – this was very grand – and his brother, Ralph, chaperoned by two aunts, took us out for tea.

When we went for walks – one prefect and four lesser mortals – we gathered nettles and dandelion leaves. The former were supposed to taste like spinach, the latter were given to us as salad; we were sure they were never washed. We ate rhubarb leaves until it was discovered they were poisonous. Britain's food shortage was already apparent.

We still wore white serge coats and skirts on Sundays and changed into silk dresses every evening. Sunday: very ancient preserved eggs for breakfast and services in the Cathedral. I was allotted a place under the pulpit. I had to sit on the edge of my pew, because if I leaned back, the pulpit toppled my sailor hat over my nose. Even on Sundays, never both jam *and* margarine, though there was an un-written law that treacle did not count as jam on the Sabbath.

A distant cousin in the Gordon Highlanders was wounded and came to Convalescent Camp at Ripon, not far from school. With Mother's permission, he approached Miss Yate Lee, the head-mistress: could he take me out to tea? Y.L. was doubtful. 'Captain Wimberley,' she said, 'I have the honour of my school to consider.' 'Miss Yate Lee,' he replied, 'I have the Honour of my Regiment.' Ernest was young, good-looking and, of course, wore the kilt. It must have been frustrating for the young members of the staff to see him wasted on a fifteen-year-old.

He was musical and knew the Cathedral organist, Dr. Moody. When Miss Yate Lee said Ernest could take me to Evensong, neither she nor I realised that our destination was the organ loft. To black out a cathedral is impossible. There was a dim light in the organ loft, space was limited. Ernest was fearful lest I should fall. What did Honour entail? Did it mean a man should not put his arms round one? The scuffle that ensued must have been disconcerting for Mr. Moody.

Twice, during the Second World War, I met Ernest at a family wedding – a middle-aged man in a top hat and morning coat who did not remember me. He lost a son in this war.

What odd things one remembers about weddings. We stayed at the Waldorf and a flying bomb demolished some buildings across the way during the night. The service in a Wren church – can't remember which; Charles was in Naval uniform, and Joy in cloth of gold, a pres-ent from some Maharajah to whom her father was financial adviser. The one beautiful bridesmaid wore a lovely delphinium-blue dress to match the flowers, a symphony of blue and gold, rather impaired by the Best Man, who wore no socks. He was Clement Attlee's nephew (Attlee was Prime Minister).

Anne rang up her father before the wedding. He didn't recognise her voice. 'Who is that?' he asked. 'Anne,' she replied. He seemed surprised. 'Which Anne?' he asked. 'Just one of your daughters,' she said, rather aggrieved that he seemed to have forgotten her.

When I went to Skellfield, there were only twenty-eight boarders. It was a new school, started by Miss Yate Lee, who had been at St.

Leonard's with a friend of my mother's. She had an M.A. from Dublin University – at that time, Oxford did not give degrees to women. There were seven members of staff and two matrons. Y.L. had her own personal maid and until the war the domestic staff was excellent.

When I first went, aged twelve, I was the youngest girl. There were four dormitories – the Yellow, the Green, the Blue and the Pink – each divided into cubicles. Prefects had windows. We went to bed in silence except on Saturday. If one girl got an 'order' mark – for running in a corridor, taking a shoe off without untying the laces, not turning a mattress, being untidy and not having a bath in her cubicle every morning (except on bath nights) – the whole dormitory suffered.

If no-one in the dormitory acquired an order mark for a whole week, we were invited to Y.L.'s drawing room on Saturday night and were allowed to talk while going to bed. This happened so rarely that I cannot remember how Y.L. entertained us on these occasions. We were not allowed to go into one another's cubicles in dormitories; one night, I heard a girl crying in the one next to mine. I broke the rule: she told me her brother had been killed in France.

Mother wrote and said that Oliver would be home on leave at half-term. 'Please tell him to be sure to wear his uniform,' I asked. They were the happiest three days I had ever known. Each morning, Radcliffe drove Oliver (in uniform!), mother and me to the foot of the Hambledon Hills, then collected us in the evening. Kepwick to Silton, Slapestones to Snilesworth. All I remember is a water splash at the foot of Kepwick bank, a haycock against which we rested before tackling a hill. Having Mother and Oliver entirely to myself.

Next term, Miss Baker instructed the Upper Fourth to write a rhymed letter as homework. 'My own dear Cousin,' mine began. 'I have written a dozen letters to you and have had no reply: I wonder why. The letters you send me I treasure with care, but I wish you would write more often, my dear. I hope that you have no obsessive objection to this sudden uncalled-for term of affection ... We went for a picnic the other day to a place in Ripley, not far away.'

I longed to tell him about this: our form mistress (not Miss Baker, but Miss Kincaird who, alas, did not stay long) invited us to tea in a cottage at Ripley and later for a walk through a bluebell wood. Someone wanted to organise games. Games in a bluebell wood! I escaped. The joy of being alone in a haze of blue mist – impossible to express in prose. Poetry certainly failed. I continue, 'There we saw some tiny frogs hopping about the marshy bogs.' True, but not inspired verse.

Oliver Lodge as a young naval surgeon in the First World War

Later I say, 'Slang by Miss Baker is forbidden, if I use more I shall be chidden.' What slang words had I used? 'Top hole' or 'ripping', perhaps. The letter ended, 'I remain, my dear Cousin, your loving J.B.' At school I was called Jane. Over seventy years later, this letter turned up among the flotsam in Oliver's safe.

Was it that term that I woke to the sound of terrific explosions and went to sleep again, to be shaken by a cross, scared prefect? There had been a roll call and no reply from me. I was abandoned on the back stairs (why should they be presumed safer than the front ones?), while the prefects went to Y.L.'s drawing room to watch a Zeppelin come down in flames. The bombs were dropped quite close to school. One of the staff read to those of us sitting on the stairs and we were provided with cocoa. A pleasant interlude, but we were annoyed that we had not been allowed to watch the Zeppelin.

When we were given a free afternoon and Y.L. asked what we would like to do, Marjorie suggested football. The storm that broke over her head was drastic. We never discovered why. At Skellfield, we played lacrosse rather than hockey in the winter terms. Sunny summer afternoons playing cricket. A poem by Marjorie, sung to the tune of 'I do like living in England':

> Oh I do like cricket at Skellfield,
> That is the game for me,
> Playing at point when Wyngrave's bat,
> And saving your life by lying down flat,
> And then they ask what the dickens you're at,
> Oh I do like cricket at Skellfield.
>
> Oh I do like cricket at Skellfield,
> That is the game for me,
> When the ball goes whizzing right past your ear,
> And Miss Lord says sweetly 'It's all right dear,
> If you just keep awake there is nothing to fear.'
> Oh I do like cricket at Skellfield.
>
> Oh I do like cricket at Skellfield,
> That is the game for me,
> When the pitch is swimming in haze and heat,
> And the ball goes slipping between your feet,
> And tempers are not what you might call sweet,
> Oh I do like cricket at Skellfield.

Sunny afternoons with the chestnut trees in flower when from a distance came the tragic sound of pipes playing 'The Flowers of the Forest', then the bugle calling the Last Post.

1991: Jane read this and I realised she'd no idea that 'The Flowers of the Forest' and the Last Post meant a military funeral.

Frank, my brother, writing to me from 'Somewhere in France', says:

> This life, combined with the firework displays at night, would be absolutely grand were it not for the shells that keep coming over. Of course it is quite interesting watching our shells knocking down the enemy trenches but it is quite a different matter when *they* start. They come over making a noise something between a baby howling and a pan of water upset on the fire and explode with a plop! bang! and then we all run like rabbits for the dugouts and not much of us is seen or heard for a bit.

After this, Frank was wounded. Discovered too young to be in the trenches, he was sent home. He promptly joined the R.A.F. and was posted to Arabia.

We still fished in school holidays. On our way to Aberdeen, we were as excited as ever when from the train we caught our first glimpse of the sea. There was a ship on the horizon; as if it were on rockers it turned turtle, only its hull remaining above water. I told Oliver when he came on leave. He said one of the terrible things – when he was transferred as full Surgeon to *H.M.S. Berwick* and they were escorting convoys to the U.S.A. – was to see people in the water and not be able to rescue them. The safety of the rest of the ships had to be considered. At school when it was my turn to choose a hymn it was always 'For those in Peril on the Sea'.

Holidays were not the same with no Martha to welcome one home with steamed chocolate pudding and chocolate sauce; no wonder I am plump today. Mother had become quartermaster of the Red Cross and wore a red dress instead of a blue one. She went to garden parties at Buckingham Palace. I must have passed an exam because I had a red cross on my apron. My chief task was to kitchen maid for a friend of Mother's who had never cooked in her life before.

Leaving school was quite a heart-rending moment. Singing 'Forty Years On' and the intimidating thought of the 'pijaw', our final interview with the headmistress, ahead. No-one ever divulged the content of this talk – in fact, I think we were not fully aware of what it was all about. I had a vague feeling she was warning me that young

Schooldays at Skellfield near Ripon

Sheona aged seventeen in a Red Cross hospital during the First World War

men had to be kept strictly at bay. Each of us acquired a fine volume of a poet of our own choice. I asked for Shelley, of whom she did not approve. Dear Y.L., I was really very fond of her and she certainly had a beneficial influence.

She told me that all my life I would regret leaving school before taking the Senior Cambridge. A friend was recovering from a nervous breakdown after this examination. I did not want to suffer this fate. Besides, there was plenty to do at the hospital and I suspect Mother and Father were pleased to have me home. I was seventeen.

We were all in the main ward when the end of the war was announced – how, and by whom, I can't remember. We stood at attention, nurses and men who were mobile, and sang 'God Save the King'. Then we went on with our work.

In 1919, Oliver was still in the Navy, surgeon in the *Curaçao*. In borrowed dress sword and epaulettes, he accompanied the Admiral to a banquet celebrating the Independence of Finland. He was thought to understand the lingo as he'd been observed talking to a Finnish doctor in a mixture of Latin and French.

Another time, he was summoned to the British Consulate in Revel, Latvia, when someone fell ill. It had been considered diplomatic to lower the Union Jack which made the building difficult to locate. As Oliver searched for his way, five German officers came towards him. To the Germans at that time, the word 'armistice' conveyed the meaning 'weapon stillstand'. They did not regard themselves as defeated and still behaved belligerently. It was impossible for an Englishman to step aside – a diplomatic 'incident' would be inconvenient to say the least. Oliver rang the bell of a house facing the pavement. A girl opened the door, recognised the situation (needless to add that she was pretty), led him to safety from the back door. Oliver reached the Consulate, the sick man was cured, the Union Jack raised.

The *Curaçao* was mined in the Baltic. Oliver performed amputations with the assistance of the young paymaster who gave an excellent anaesthetic, he said.

After the surrender of the German fleet, Oliver took Mother and me on board one of their sad ships. There was no feeling of jubilation, only thankfulness that it was they who had been defeated, not us. That night there was a dance at Dovercourt. I wore my first evening dress; it had transparent sleeves and Mother made me wear an elbow length woollen vest underneath because I had a cold. She did allow me to powder my nose for the first time; she powdered her own as well but then rubbed it off, as she always did.

It's not only grief that's like a river in spate, ideas swirl in the confines of the mind.

It was here that the typewriter ribbon wore out. Asking Rick or Paul to fit a new one is like asking Mr. Marconi to change a lamp bulb. Their customers include The National Trust. All computer men are young, six foot four, handsome, charming and as difficult to capture as eels. Not surprising, what is £3.50 compared with millions? Paul is engaged: what must it be like marrying someone from 'Star Trek' or 'Things to Come'!

──────── Chapter Two ────────

GROWING UP

War over. School clothes discarded. Long skirts, hair in a bun, more bother than plaits, hair pins all over the place …

A cheque for £24 from Father, 'Your dress allowance,' he said, 'take it to Barclays.' I had never been to a bank with Mother or with Father, but I'd played in the garden with the Bank Manager's daughter. I suppose I should have said, 'I want to open an account.' Instead I stuttered, 'Will you cheque this cash.' The bank clerk laughed. He must have given me a cheque book because I wrote one out for £24 and took it across the road to the Midland, which had a Manager and no clerks.

The years after the war were an odd mixture. Sometimes no help in the house. Fires to light, floors to scrub. No hoover, no central heating. On the other hand, there were dances. Dances at people's houses, Hunt Balls, *Thé Dansants*, dances in the Town Hall, dances at Raby Castle.

RABY CASTLE

It was said a coach and four
Could drive through the great door.
We arrived in a Morris Eight – a trifle early.
Host, hostess and house party had reached port
And dessert, table glittering with candelabra,
Finger bowls and silver.

'The ballroom presented a scene of dazzling splendour,'
Said the *Darlington and Stockton Times* next morning.

Dowagers, magnificent in tiaras and white satin
Salvaged from wardrobes unopened for war years,
(No longer ladies' maids to repair the ravages of time),
Retaining their dignity despite a battery of safety pins
Supporting gaping seams. Lorgnettes raised they surveyed
The young foxtrotting, one-stepping, to a Clifford Essex Band.

Boar's head, oysters and champagne. Winding stone stairs
Leading to secluded spots for sitting out. Four o'clock and
Breakfast of devilled bones. A moment on the battlements.
Starlight. Snow seeping through silver slippers.

No driving tests in those days. But I had to learn to change a wheel, clean the sparking plugs and blow down a tube inside the bonnet (I don't know what that was for). If one sucked instead of blowing, it meant a mouthful of petrol. Changing gear on hills was tricky. The Stellite was a minute Wolseley, old and temperamental. Father had bought it because it used less petrol in the war. I took Mother 'calling' on new people who now lived in most of the old houses. One house that had once had no bathrooms now had seven – and a golf course! 'Calling' was awful.

If you want to know what Father was like, read Trollope's *Dr. Thorne*, only the Doctor, as far as I can remember, was a good deal better off than we were.

The first time I went anywhere on my own was when Mrs. Gott invited me to Talgarth in Wales. I had never before had a maid to unpack for me or had my evening dress laid out on my bed. I did not dare to challenge her choice. Driving round the estate in the dog cart with Mrs. Gott, whose husband had been a great friend of Father's, was interesting. She wanted to improve the stock and land, not only her own but that of the whole county. She belonged to the generation which gave to Medical Schools, Libraries, Churches. She dreamt of an Utopian World. Her nephew, General Gott, was killed in the Second World War.

Mrs. Gott owned several miles of the Dovey and I was supposed to catch salmon, and didn't. The head keeper had been stoned by poachers and was in hospital. The estate carpenter who ghillied for me was morose and I had never fished a tidal river before. At the end of the day, he led me home through what was obviously private land. 'It's a right of way,' he said. We walked past a house, then down a long drive. When I told Mrs. Gott she was dismayed. A lawsuit had just been concluded and the landowner had lost the case. My ghillie was crowing over the outcome. Next Sunday I was taken to the owner in order to apologise. He was charming and sympathetic.

From Wales, I joined Mother and Father and met Grafton. I saw him from my window as I was dressing for dinner. He was crossing the bridge over the Aira. I fell in love. From school, Grafton had gone straight into the army, so he was older than the average Oxford undergraduate. (He had been in Roxborough's sixth form and was later asked to become a house master at Stowe.)

At that time, Ian Campbell, the heir apparent, was about seventeen and the Duke of Argyll was endeavouring to reform and initiate him. Grafton, who was tutoring the local Bank Manager's son, was regarded as a suitable companion for Ian. Grafton's great-grandfather had been Regent for the King of Spain (it would require an historian to verify this!). An uncle was one of the Lords of the Admiralty. Grafton was a superior young man and in great demand by all the young women who were scattered about Scotland at that time…

Next year at a Commem Ball, Grafton asked me to marry him; if I said no we would never meet again. As I didn't say yes he decided he would ask me again in the summer vac.

When Oliver was near I lived in a haze of bliss – but he did not ask me to marry him. Oh! to be middle-aged and feelings would surely be less intense …

Grafton encouraged me to read *The Canterbury Tales*, Malory's *Le Morte d'Arthur*, Donne, Herbert, Dryden, Pope. Oliver on his way to see me learned Keats's 'Ode on a Grecian Urn', many Shakespeare sonnets and Tennyson's 'Ulysses'. One of them gave me a hat, the other a set of golf clubs that arrived by the same post. Father, justly irate because I was uncertain, capricious and moody, accused me of being like a film star. He could not think of anything worse to say about anyone.

February 1989: Grandson Angus has been skiing in Poland. His letter is triggering another spot of time…

I went to Switzerland with friends. They asked me to bring an extra man. I invited Grafton but, when he couldn't come, suggested Oliver. This is an extract from a letter to Mother:

Hotel Schweizerhof: Lenzerheide: January 4th 1924

Boulogne – land of any kind seemed paradise – found Eric, Ian and Betty on the train.

I wish I could draw you a picture of what we looked like last night. We put our suitcases upright on the floor, level with the seats, and lay full length. My feet tucked into Eric's neck, Oliver's on Agnes's shoulder and in my ear. If we didn't sleep like tops, we had a night's rest, though awakened at intervals by fierce ticket collectors flashing red lanterns onto us … Arrived at Basle a few hours late, looking like nothing on earth, perfectly filthy, and my hair completely down.

Saturday. Our adventures began at Chur. To begin with, porters and everyone who was supposed to be looking after our luggage appeared to be completely off their heads. To make matters worse, could only converse in German. When our luggage was found, an officious little man who seemed to be in charge refused to believe it was ours. We could not get our porter to verify our statement as he had gone off duty. When Eric and Oliver ventured into his den, he shooed them out and threatened them with the police. So we spent an hour losing each other, our heads and our tempers.

Later the cause of the confusion was revealed. The worst avalanche for forty years had occurred that morning. Our road was blocked and the telephone poles down. However, we at length managed to get hold of a sleigh. At least we thought we had, but some other people going to Lenzerheide appeared to think it was theirs. A ten-franc note put this little matter right, but the other people were furious.

We set off gaily with our bells ringing – the bells sounded simply ripping.

As it was dusk, our driver stopped and asked whether the road was safe. Some said no, others were doubtful, but they all seemed to think it risky.

The road was narrow – hardly passing room. We met very few other sleighs but when we did it took about twenty minutes and much shouting in German before we could pass. We got to the avalanche in about two hours. There were men with lanterns to guide us and it really was somewhat thrilling. There was just enough light to see a steep precipice on one side, with broken telegraph poles and fir trees and hardly room for us. Men swinging lanterns added a certain picturesqueness to the scene and in any case the fear of being seasick is much worse than the prospect of fifty avalanches.

The people whose sleigh we had annexed were close behind us and, as they had fewer passengers, we traded Agnes for one of their suitcases.

We stopped at a little inn and had lovely hot chocolate while the horses fed. Soon after this, the real thrill of the evening occurred. One horse stepped into a drift. For a moment we were balanced and then over we went, horses and all. We had some difficulty in extricating ourselves. My ankle was a bit bruised but otherwise no damage was done. The man thought one horse was hurt but he found it was all right. We arrived at the hotel at ten o'clock, instead of four.

One lives in breeches all day. We spent Saturday morning hiring and waxing skis. The luggage came in the afternoon and we tried skiing. The first tiny hill was terrifying. I fell after a

Skiing in Switzerland, 1924 (note the puttees and leather boots)

couple of yards, blocking the whole path, and could not get up. Agnes hauled me to my feet. The second time I fell, a strange – and probably beautiful (but I was too unhappy to notice his appearance) – young man gave me a helping hand. The rest of the time I stumbled about – Oliver got on splendidly.

This morning we started directly after breakfast and climbed by ourselves to the top of a high mountain (a slight slope) and tried coming down. It was soft snow and hard work, so we soon joined the others. Again, Oliver excelled and everyone was filled with admiration. Last night we danced.

Yesterday we achieved practically the impossible and climbed well over two thousand feet on a roll and a half, two cups of tea and a fit of pique.

After breakfast Agnes had informed us that they were going on an expedition, but thought it might be too much for me. After this, all Oliver and I could do was to say that perhaps it would be better for us to practise a little rather than keep them back. So the two of us set off with a camera and a flask of whisky. It was a perfect day and our objective a small gap in the mountains, a goal none but experts would dream of attempting. We tacked up the hill and it seemed so easy and jolly that we simply had to go on.

There was only one unpleasantly thrilling moment when I slipped on the steepest part of the slope that the sun had not reached. It was hard ice. I clung for all I was worth to one ski stick, which felt very insecure, and tried not to look down till Oliver came to the rescue. It was difficult for him because there was no hold for skis. I felt like a fly trying to climb up a tumbler. He clung on to me till I dug some sort of foothold, and we were soon out of danger.

Once we got to the top, it was glorious. Ranges and ranges of mountains all around us. We sat on a rock gazing and had a good pull at the whisky – by the way, we are longing to know if it was neat or otherwise. Do tell me when you write. Later we were joined by a charming damsel and a young man who displayed the utmost tact and sympathy by offering to take our photograph, and we took theirs.

I was prepared to be terrified coming down; it looked impossible. But by zig-zagging across and across, it was easy! It took longer than expected. The first person we met was Herr Brenn – the proprietor of the Hotel Schweizerhof. We had expected the triumphant return of the intrepid adventurers. It *was* an achievement. After five minutes of Herr Brenn, we felt like a couple of naughty children. It seems that a search party was about to set off, and hot bottles and brandy were in readiness. Whether the brandy was for us or for the search party was never made clear. We saw nothing of it.

It was of course very inconsiderate of us. But hitherto our party had not expressed the slightest interest in us or our movements. Between ourselves, I think their feelings were those of annoyance at our achieving more than they had, rather than anxiety as to our safety. Anyway, our colds are better. Skiing has no more terror for me and I'm cured of funk.

The Christiana and the Telemark –
We practised them upon the nursery slope,
Watching our more experienced friends embark
On expeditions far beyond our scope.

The day came when they said to Oliver,
'You are proficient now, you come with us.
Sheona? There is the Pro to minister
To her deficiencies, you needn't fuss.'

O. thanked them, said that he would stay with me:
Looking thoughtfully at the Lenzerhorn
He bound with care a rope upon each ski,
No mentor to advise or to forewarn.

And off we set, all in the dazzling snow –
I didn't recognise 'O. Symptom' then
That meant, 'There's something to be conquered, go
Surmount it, though the odds be one in ten.'

And we achieved the summit, God knows how!
The only sound the beating of the raven's wing
Above the towering peaks, while far below
Unknown to us, dismay was deepening.

When we came down to earth again,
Herr Brenn, in billowing cloak and broad brimmed hat,
Advanced towards us to explain
We'd broken every rule of Sport, and that
A search party, at his request,
Was now assembled in the Schweizerhof
And would have demanded, at the very least,
A cheque for fifty pounds, had they set off.

I chose to wear my white and silver dress.
The rival Inn – The Kurhaus – held by chance
A gala night. Our feat 'foolhardiness'?
Aggrieved, we crossed the moon-lit street to dance.
We danced, we hoped, we dreamed,
Dreams of no substance,
Lofty as unscalable mountains,
Deep as insoluble snow,

To music of a string quartet,
The glow of, from here and there,
A sympathetic glance;
Aloft in our star-lit world we were
Oblivious to the dancers down below.

The married couples went up in the lift.
How enviable the lot we did not share.
Thoughts unexpressed, yet again aware the drift,
Each wishing each 'good night' upon the stair.

After Switzerland, I stayed with Aunt Katy in London and met Grafton and told him I could not marry him. He made me promise neither to see nor write to him or to Oliver for three months. I cried myself to sleep every night and at last in utter despair decided to become a spinster. Or on second thoughts, a matron at a boys' school.

I can laugh now but being young is pretty tragic. I really do feel awful about Grafton because he was so charming and carefree when I met him; now when I read his last letters (which I promised faithfully to burn), he sounds so sad. It would have been good to remain friends and to have seen him as happily married as I was.

Did we take love more seriously in those days or is life for everyone a series of mountain top delights or depths of misery?

There! A difficult piece of the jigsaw in place. The advantage of a jigsaw rather than a book is that only the surface is on view ...

At Easter, Father called Oliver to Northallerton to perform an emergency operation and somehow or other we became engaged! Father, Mother and I were about to set off for Aberdeenshire. That holiday was sheer magic. Even the trout were infected; I only had to arrive at a pool and the fish rose to my fly in a manner that was daft, making Father say, 'It is a pity to think of marriage just when you are becoming an Angler.' I was bringing back baskets better than his and his were known to be the best, as far as the Don was concerned. It seemed to have nothing to do with skill, it was just that the river became transformed. It was catching fish in heaven where there is no pain and St. Peter – himself a fisherman – rejoicing.

One day at breakfast, a telegram came for me. 'Marry me in Edinburgh on Thursday,' it said. I handed it to Mother. She made no observation, but stalked out of the dining room. When she returned, having crossed the road to the shop that sold corsets, violins and had

Sheona and Oliver on their wedding-day, 24th June 1924

a telephone, she said, 'I have sent an answer.' 'What did you say?' I asked. 'Certainly not,' was her reply. 'I signed it Sheona.' It transpired that the telegram was prompted by a hospital appointment in Bradford with a salary of £600 a year.

We were married in June 1924.

We went to London for our honeymoon and stayed at Jules, which was destroyed in the blitz. The nice thing about it was that it was next door to Floris; Oliver's choice of scent forever after was 'Wild Hyacinth'. Oliver was reading Law and Eating Dinners at the Inner Temple, so we could combine business with pleasure. Daisy Taylor, with whom we fished the Don – her father had taken the Castle Forbes water – took us to *Romeo and Juliet* and to watch polo at Hurlingham. We dined with Daisy and her husband, General Taylor, who commanded the 13th Hussars and had fought at Omdurman. I think it was he who had chosen Jules for us, because it had the reputation of being the best place to dine in town. What made an impression on Oliver was the dover sole we had for breakfast in bed and the wardrobe that, when opened, revealed a spectacular bath complete with hot and cold water which descended at his feet to his delight and surprise.

What more can one say about a honeymoon?

―――― Chapter Three ――――

WEST RIDING

Halifax was chosen for us as a base because my father-in-law had consulting rooms there and Oliver an honorary appointment at the Infirmary. When Father saw the house, he said it had a very good back. In fact it was the front he was looking at!

Granddaughter Sue has just bought a house in Pietermaritzburg with a veranda and swimming pool. Her husband, Yunus, is aghast at the thought of such an unsuitable setting for a man of his political persuasion. Her letter sparks off another spot of time ...

I was prepared to share a shed with Oliver, but I could not live with the fireplace in the sitting room. The discovery of old Dutch tiles remains a mystery. Never again could I find the shop. The owner had said, 'No one here wants the likes of these.' For once, I was adamant. I had my Dutch tiles.

Sheona and daughter Anne with the Dutch-tiled fireplace in Halifax

Oliver provided the two essentials for a happy marriage, a baby grand and a double bed; Mother a bureau, an oak chest, a portfolio of old prints and all my nursery furniture. The doll's chest of drawers a year later was exactly right for baby clothes. The Staffordshire dogs, Spot and Dot, came with me and a tea caddy that contains love letters and has a key that has long been lost.

Why should the Dutch tiles remain a landmark? In my life, I have made three unaided decisions. The choice of parents, a husband and those tiles. Oh! and a pair of silver slippers. The only other purchase I made without asking Mother was a hat; I don't count that as she wouldn't let me wear it.

Another magic thing about those tiles was the unreality of that time. A magic shop that sold magic tiles that could never be found again.

How fortunate it is when spots of time are all the colours of the rainbow ... and now ...

Winter 1991: For Kurds on the borders of Turkey and Iran, nothing but starvation and disease, fear and despair. How can heaven be heaven when a planet seethes with suffering?

I dreamed last night I was totally blind.

When I learned to read I discovered at the back of *Through the Looking Glass* one of the few poems Mother had not read to me. It ended, 'Life, what is it but a dream?' I hadn't quite believed in the Walrus and the Carpenter and Jabberwocky, but I did hope that this might be true.

To be with Oliver was all that mattered. Oliver had no 'off days', but when work took him to the country, the operations over, we had hours of bliss discovering Wharfedale. It was only when we were driving back to Halifax and blue sky was left behind and a dark pall of black smoke lay ahead, that the heart sank.

To Mother, the West Riding was still beyond the pale. 'You can't wear that West Riding hat here!' she would say. It's not surprising that a Halifax friend told me, 'When you first came here, I thought you were the silliest woman I had ever met.' Wives of other doctors must have imagined I was half-witted when they asked, 'Are you L.G.I. or G.R.I.?' and I had no idea what they meant. Nearly all doctors' wives had been nurses in those days.

Anne tells me now that L.G.I. was Leeds General Infirmary but what was G.R.I.?

We became members of Queen's Tennis Club and, because we were ashamed of our bad play, we also joined another one in Leeds in order to be coached, unaware that it was the County Players' club. That our motive was misunderstood was not revealed until years later.

Mother had found for us a starchy and very superior maid who liked my father-in-law, and daily reduced me to tears. A shabbily dressed man came to the front door. She sent him round to the back. He was our only millionaire patient.

We could marry, Father had said, on one condition: that, even if Oliver could not manage it, I should join him and Mother in Scotland twice a year. In September, I posted my heavy luggage, boots and waders in advance. On the day of my departure, I sent a telegram: 'Impossible'. My parents were disappointed; Edith (the waspish maid) was furious. Her plans – I wonder what they were – disrupted. More tears on my part.

When finally Edith departed, Aunt Madge's May came to us for a time, which was sheer bliss. May was an absolute darling and had a mania for cleanliness. Once, having produced tea for callers (callers arrived at twenty to four and departed a quarter of an hour later, but these had come from a distance and had been persuaded to stay), she decided to tidy the false roof above the upstairs drawing room. The callers were elderly and very correct. They were surprised when there was a shriek and a pair of black stockinged legs broke through the ceiling just over their heads. Another caller once asked me, 'Do you believe in a late Easter?', a question that hitherto had not entered my mind. She added, 'Does your husband drink?' Can she really have said this?

It had never occurred to me to wonder what it would be like to be the wife of a surgeon. Father visited his patients and his surgery was far from the house. I had not even met a telephone before. Now I had to make appointments, deal with emergencies and provide solace if required when Oliver, caught up by unexpected operations, kept patients waiting. We were only to acquire a secretary some years later. With the arrival of Anne, bathtime and yells coincided with consulting hours.

It was a relief when we moved to Green Leas in 1931, but there was still a consulting room with patients waiting and Anne still yelled at bathtime. We could see the Pennines in the distance and larks soared and sang overhead.

I don't think I was ever conscious of loneliness, but I remember seeing people greet one another in shops and feeling rather envious.

One day as I walked to the town, a tram passed me going in the opposite direction and someone waved. It was Lorna. I turned and pursued that tram until it was out of sight. The idea of looking up someone's name in a telephone directory did not occur to me. I still regarded the telephone as a hurdle to be tackled. Lorna, of course, discovered where we lived. 'Heath Hall' sounded rather grand and when she saw it, she seemed as surprised as Father had been on his first visit.

Lorna Cresswell altered my life. She knew Northallerton and knew my parents, so she took me under her wing. She was beautiful and social and launched me into local society. Had she not appeared, would I have ever known anyone? She gathered round her folk from every corner of the country. What odd things one remembers – 'After accepting an invitation to dinner,' she told me, 'find out if it is black tie or white.' At home, white ties were worn only for dances. We were on call even at dinner parties (they were mostly black, not white, tie ones) and when we went to the cinema a message would flash on the screen, 'Mr. Lodge wanted at the Infirmary immediately.'

If the Royal Halifax Infirmary had a special corner in the jigsaw, here is a piece that seems to fit. On one occasion, I was a victim, having had a major operation. In the next cubicle, a young nurse was thought to be dying. Matron, Sister, all the nurses were in tears. In fact, she recovered before I did and came and talked to me. She had never thought about religion, she said, nor had she ever been to church, but she knew now there was no such thing as death, because she had seen her grandparents and other people standing, with arms outstretched, waiting to welcome her. The next time I saw her, she was Sister of the children's ward and I remember thinking 'lucky children'. She was absurdly young to be a Sister, but I have seldom met anyone with such an air of serenity, confidence and happiness.

To return to Lorna: she it was who, when I was having mysterious pains, said, 'You are about to have a baby.' I explained that I was having it at the Rutson Hospital, Northallerton, in two weeks' time, with Miss Osborne and Miss Hirst (Matron and Sister) and Father in attendance. The cot with yellow curtains and all the baby clothes were there in readiness. In spite of this, Lorna summoned the doctor. Because I was the wife of Oliver and therefore must know what I was talking about, he believed that I was suffering from a little colic.

At 2.00 a.m. the pains were really bad. I tried to rouse Oliver, but he turned over, fast asleep. I went down to the kitchen where the black telephone hung on the wall. Father had acquired one nine months before. 'Father,' I said, 'I think I'm going to have the baby.'

'Have the waters broken?' he asked. What on earth did he mean? At that moment, I knew. It was like standing in the pool beneath the Force of Callunan.

At 6 a.m. Gus, an unmarried aunt who had been staying at Dunston House, arrived in a taxi. 'Where is the doctor?' she asked. 'Where is the nurse?' Oliver was still asleep (I always felt his patients needed him wide awake, and never disturbed him unduly). Aunt Gus summoned the G.P. and two district midwives who were wonderful.

For the first time in his life, Oliver was late at St. Luke's Hospital. Anne had got entangled with the cord. Oliver sprinkled chloroform on a handkerchief. At the end, I must have taken a good whiff because I remember waking to hear what I thought was a puppy squealing at the foot of the bed. (When, during my next pregnancy, Anne was to ask me how babies were born, I was unable to enlighten her, much to her frustration.)

Oliver had been the last obstetrician to have a hansom cab at his disposal for home deliveries. The doctor was, as I have said, an experienced practitioner. How ever did I manage to delude them both? But parents were infallible. If parents said I was having a baby two weeks hence, then of course I was. One other thought has at this minute occurred to me. I really did want to have that baby at home.

Acquiring Nurse Hirst was akin to entering a son for Eton on conception: her babies were superior. She carried 'her' babies in her arms for the first three weeks, as 'this was better for them than a pram'. She was already booked so we had Nurse Vincent. When Nurse Vincent arrived on the scene, she decreed that the baby was not to be fed for twenty-four hours, then every four hours on the dot – not two minutes before or after. Three weeks later we were allowed to go to the Pictures and had to leave Harold Lloyd dangling on the edge of a precipice. I did so want to see how that film ended. Before nurse departed, she showed me how to bath the baby, which was a terrifying experience. It was so slippery. Oliver did it without turning a hair.

The baby – it wasn't quite Anne yet – wore a vest, a barracoat (made of fine flannel), a lawn petticoat and a lawn dress twice as long as herself. They had to be starched and ironed and the dress had a ribbon slotted through it. Sheets and pillowcases too had to be ironed and the pram must always be spotless. There was little time to enjoy a baby, but at twenty-five minutes to six – before its bath – it was allowed to lie on the bed and kick. Apart from this allotted time, babies preferred to be tightly wrapped up; 'like being in the womb,' said Nurse Vincent. She tut-tutted when she found Anne in the carry cot on the piano, being played to by Oliver.

Nurse Vincent left after six weeks. While Anne slept, I knelt beside the cot and doted; at all other times I followed the rules laid down by Truby King. We were conscientious, even if Anne never had any doubts about our ineptitude. When the baby was old enough to discard long clothes for (still starched) short ones, a white drugget was procured to allow the baby a little more freedom on the floor. The drugget was a woolly rug, which May said I had to have. On no account must Anne proceed beyond this onto an unhygienic carpet. Next came weaning and hours spent over the blanching of brains and the sieving of fruit and vegetables, only to see Anne send them flying in all directions under the disapproving eye of Papa-in-law.

Are children always wiser than their parents? I begin to think now – for the first time – that I managed to wrap myself, and Oliver too, in an escapist (but lovely) never-never world. It didn't dawn on either of us that children should go to school. Anne could tot up the price of petrol faster than Oliver. I didn't try.

My mother, however, had planned Anne's schooling with considerable care, but the scheme was frustrated. First she was invited to climb the Victoria plum tree at Dunston House to watch Mrs. Lord's children at play in the garden over the wall; next, Roger Lord was invited to tea. He was a year older than Anne and a contented pupil in his mother's school. The visit was returned. His toy farmyard was impressively mechanised and had corrugated paper for ploughed fields. Anne's farm had more baby animals, and there was real hay for them to eat. They played at dominoes and spillikins. She thought she would like to sit next to Roger at school, and play with the other children under the next door garden pear trees.

The heralded first school day came. Mrs. Lord gave Anne a book and suggested that she should 'learn the alphabet'. Anne knew her ABC backwards and forwards and could read single words, but had no idea how one 'learned' anything, and in any case, what was an alphabet and, even if one had known, how did one 'learn' it? In her six years, she had never done anything until she was quite certain of getting it right.

There was only one course of action – escape. This she did when Mrs. Lord became absorbed with a pupil at the far end of the room. Creeping to the huge locked front door, she wrestled with the bolts, key and chain, shut the door softly behind her, fled to the Dunston House door, hammering the knocker, pealing the bell, shrieking in desperation to be folded into safe arms and resuscitated with pink and white iced buns.

Perhaps this was why school was forgotten for the next eighteen months. When she was seven, it was pointed out that education was compulsory, so she went to Mrs. Dudley's little day school in Halifax. I suffered: homework! The name 'Bolingbroke' and the years between 1455 and 1486 still fill me with dismay. On the other hand, all was well for Anne. Asked to read *Tales from Troy and Greece*, she knew how to pronounce Telemachus, Persephone and Menelaus. She survived to go on to a boarding prep school in Harrogate and in due course to Wycombe Abbey.

Anne could not see why Mrs. Dudley should complain about her absentmindedness. Was not her Papa absentminded? Had he not congratulated her mother on the delicious luncheon he supposed he had eaten before it had even emerged from the oven? His mind was occupied with higher matters.

Indeed, both parents seemed to have a complete disregard for what, to them, were the minor practicalities of life. When she went to Wycombe Abbey, she was left to travel two hundred miles to school without provision of money for a ticket. Her House Mistress was surprised to be presented with a Health Certificate, duly punched by several ticket collectors who had not studied the nature of the document presented to them for her safe passage by rail.

Children are critical of their own – and other people's – parents. Oliver, Anne told me, looked too young to be a parent. 'What about me?' I asked. 'Oh,' said Anne, 'they think you more suitable.'

TO ANNE: EASTER 1983

1925
Slotting blue ribbons
Through starched petticoats;
Blanching brains
Because they were good for babies,
According to Truby King
And other people's nannies.

1961
You in your turn
With your children
Feeding 'on demand',
Never saying 'No',
Never saying
'Put those toys away'.

1983
The young maintaining
That all you and I have done
Is WRONG,
Our thoughts and attitudes
Not merely naive; plain stupid.

W.O.L. says –
Thinking of you,
Angus, Jane and Sue –
That time spent
Blanching brains
Has surely proved
Profitable.

In 1926, Oliver had not yet given up the thought of combining Medicine and Law. Eating Dinners led us to London – a good stepping-off place for the Continent. I suspect Oliver did not reveal his plans beforehand lest I should rebel. They always took me by surprise. 'What do you say about flying to Paris tomorrow?'

Had we passports? Had he arranged a flight, money, an hotel? The last two questions were answered. Banks were closed so General Taylor had cashed a cheque for him at the 'In and Out' club, and Daisy had suggested an hotel in the Rue de Cambon. My contribution was to take us both to the eight o'clock service before setting off.

It seemed tranquil: a solitary plane in a large green field, no fuss, no air hostess. We clambered aboard. There were three other passengers. I looked out of the window; it seemed that we were about to set off. One thing I had observed – a notice saying 'Be sure to bolt the door'. The door was open. I shut and bolted it. Just in time, I thought. The plane was beginning to taxi across the runway. All at once there was a fearful commotion: people appearing from nowhere, shouting, gesticulating. The plane stopped. The navigator arose from the cockpit, strode to the door and unbolted it. I had locked out the pilot.

I told this story the other day and a flying man explained that in those days it was customary for the pilot to leap aboard in a nonchalant manner at the last moment. By the time we got to Paris – it took two hours and was terribly bumpy – the pilot had recovered his temper and we shared a taxi with him and the navigator from Le Bourget to Paris.

INTERIOR OF IMPERIAL AIRWAYS PASSENGER
AEROPLANE, ACCOMMODATION, 20 PASSENGERS

A flying visit to Paris, 1926

The first evening, we decided to go to the Opera. We hadn't booked seats. When we arrived, they were half way through the first act. Our taxi driver said he would take us to what had been one of Edward VII's favourite haunts. We imagined this to be a cabaret. We weren't enthusiastic, but the taxi driver was insistent. He took us to a house in a quiet street and rang the bell.

Five years in the Navy and Oliver still an innocent abroad! He was as surprised as I was to be led by Madame to a very peculiar room, 'The King's favourite,' she said. But if we were not satisfied, perhaps we would prefer this one. It had a four-poster bed with a looking glass top. Oliver explained in French that we had been misled. She chose to think that we were hard to please. She led us from room to room, eventually clapping her hands, upon which a score of naked maidens materialised. Even I in a state of acute embarrassment could not help seeing that they were lovely, of every nationality and colour.

Oliver and Madame appeared to be arguing about money. Oliver was not prepared to pay for this unrequested entertainment. As a compromise, Madame suggested champagne to appease the young ladies. When Oliver turned down the idea, they surged forward like a pack of hyenas, uttering ear-splitting howls. The next thing I remember is being locked in a cage entirely lined by mirrors. In vain, we searched for a hidden spring. To end one's life in a looking-glass cage! We might be traced to Rue de Cambon, but no further. The disposal of a couple of corpses would be no problem in Paris. After what seemed an interminable time we were released. The taxi was waiting. England seemed very safe! I have never dared to tell this story before.

November 1991: 'The King in Love' is not a book I would have chosen for myself. I depend now on large print books and the kindness of the librarian. But in this book I have discovered that this place we were taken to was indeed patronised by Edward VII, so the taxi driver was telling the truth. It was called Le Chabanais, and his 'curious double decker chair' was recently sold for £20,000.

So that was my first holiday with Oliver after our marriage. The next year, I thought we were going to the New Forest, or Devon. I'd packed fishing things. When we got to London, he told me he'd booked tickets to the Riviera. I burst into tears at the thought of going to the Riviera in boots, brogues and heavy tweeds. Oliver sweetly asked, 'Where can you go with boots and brogues?' I said that, clad like that, the only possible place was Germany. So we chose Freiburg. Oliver went to the hospital – he always worked during our holidays. We trekked across the Feldberg. Weeks later, we read that a schoolmaster and walking party lost their lives on this same walk.

We were living on the edge of an era about to topple: the age of Noël Coward and the Bright Young Things. We didn't know this, of course. Oliver and I belonged – as our parents did – to the Barrie period. Angry Young Men were in their cradles. We had the best Police Force and Civil Service in the world, we didn't lock our doors, trains were never late, porters found one a corner seat facing the engine, and one could park a car anywhere.

Bond Street was like Jane Austen's Bath. How leisurely life seemed to be on the occasions when we went to London for meetings at the Royal Society of Medicine. These had come about through Sir St. Clair Thompson, who was doyen of the Ear, Nose and Throat world. When we were with him, we met foreign professors 'who had operated upon the crowned heads of Europe'! There were probably already fewer of these around ... With Sir St. Clair we dined and danced at the Bulgaria. My dancing wasn't up to his standard. He said I should have lessons.

Was it because we'd had the war to end all wars that we felt carefree and certain that for everyone things were going to get better and better? We lived frugally at home, but in London stayed at The Dorchester, Claridges, The Hyde Park Hotel and then eventually always at The Basil Street. We didn't feel guilty about dining at Quaglino's or at Scott's, which in any case weren't outrageously expensive. Besides, we met interesting people: one of them was the inventor of the 'cat's whisker', which was something to do with radio.

We were fortunate too in knowing Daisy Taylor. Had it not been for her, Oliver would not have skated on the Grosvenor House ice rink with Cecilia Colledge, an Olympic champion, and with a lady-in-waiting to Queen Mary. General Taylor had been with the King and Queen in India and Queen Mary had offered to help him choose a birthday present for Daisy. It was one he couldn't afford but it would have seemed ungracious to say so. Young Kent and Gloucester weren't allowed cars, so they practised on Daisy's. It was exciting to hear about this glamorous world.

We also went to stay at Mrs. Gott's. Each bedroom had its own dressing room and we did not dare to contravene custom by sharing a bed. One night there was an almighty crash. All the men of the house party rushed to the top of the stairs. The great gong had fallen. Mrs. Gott asked Oliver to wait until all the men had returned to their respective dressing rooms before putting out the light. Oliver had to find the way to his room in the dark. He grasped the brass bed knobs and vaulted onto a pair of bony knees. In horror, he fled to me. The next morning at breakfast his clinical eye identified their owner, the daughter of a Bishop. We did not tell Mrs. Gott this story until years later.

In the West Riding, a group of sophisticated folk were rehearsing *Hay Fever* with a professional producer. My only acting experience was in a Missionary play at school, when I had four words to say, so I was flattered at being given the part of the maid. The drama that ensued at rehearsals and long after the play was over would have delighted Noël Coward.

Chapter Four

TRAVELS IN THE THIRTIES

Germany

In 1934, when motoring through the Black Forest, we gave a lift to one of Hitler's Storm Troopers – a nice young man. I remember saying, 'You seem to like this Hitler of yours.' 'Like him! I would die for him! He's given us something to live for!' was his reply. We parted with lots of 'Heil Hitlers' and salutes.

In April 1936, in a letter to Anne from Munich, I say:

> People look happy and fit, the girls very brown ... We went to a heavenly village in the mountains to see Neuschwanstein, a castle built by King Ludwig. We weren't allowed to go round until the guide had finished his lunch. While we were waiting, your papa disappeared. I sat on the battlements gazing at the Alps and becoming a little anxious. A nice man came and told me his life story in a mixture of German and English. Then the guides and lots of other people arrived and demanded money. All I could do was to wring my hands and say I had lost 'meine manner'. They all looked frightfully suspicious and said they'd none of them seen 'eine manner'. I was at my wits' end when Daddy strolled up, looking pleased with himself and not a bit repentant, saying he'd had such a long (nearly an hour) conversation, all in German, with a delightful little woman who sold postcards.
>
> Some day I wish you would have German lessons with me. Whenever I lose your papa, I get so agitated as he always has the money and the passports and I can only gesticulate helplessly until he comes to the rescue. I believe he likes Germany because there he has a comparatively silent wife.

This happened in other countries. In a train on the way to Florence, Oliver having leapt out of the carriage at Milan, two sympathetic Swiss women made me learn a long sentence in Italian. I hadn't any idea what it meant. When Oliver returned, I repeated it to him. The Swiss ladies roared with laughter at his expression and translated my speech for me – 'I have lost my husband. He has my money and my passport and I am looking for someone to console me.'

Sheona and Oliver at the Brandenburg Gate, Berlin, 1936

Oliver learned the languages of the countries we were to visit while scrubbing up, his book propped above the taps. In the pre-penicillin era, hands had to be washed scrupulously for a minimum of ten minutes before each operation.

Extract from a letter, Hotel Adlon, Unter den Linden, Berlin 1936:

> Streets packed, everyone waiting to see Hitler. No-one in the Adlon appeared to be particularly interested. An Edinburgh professor and I were. I can't think why we were arrested. Oliver fortunately had seen us rush out of the door and followed. A few words from him in their own lingo and we were passed courteously from one policeman to another with the magic words, *'Ausländer, Adlon'*.

The Costa Rican Ambassador asked us to see 'The Night Life' of Berlin with him, but we got little further than the roof garden of the Eden, where we could hear lions roaring as we danced.

We passed the flying ground as Hitler was stepping into his plane ... It is terrible fun meeting people who are internationally famous, especially when they are sweet into the bargain. I adore having my hand kissed.

One wonders now if any of these famous people were Hitler's minions; that was still an age of innocence.

Sweden 1938

I've said nothing yet about the reason for our jaunts abroad. It's not easy because, in the realms of surgery, I am more ignorant than the average being who reads with interest of transplants and other miracles of science. I still turn off the television at the sight of blood or violence.

Oliver was asked by a fellow E.N.T. man to go with him to Sweden. He would plan everything, he said. Oliver began to learn the language. The train from Gothenburg to Stockholm was as clean as the Rhinegold Express. A handsome white-coated woman walked up and down, dusting tables and windows. Another stood outside a spotless loo with clean towels and fresh soap. In the centre of Stockholm there were ships' masts and gulls, and in no time the city merged into countryside not unlike the West Coast of Scotland. It seemed to me a near approach to Utopia. No apparent poverty, education excellent, a high degree of intelligence and everyone owning a house or a cottage in the country. Later I was told that there were more divorces there than anywhere else.

We dined with Professor Hölmgrun and met a Hungarian surgeon with an actress wife who had recently played Juliet, but was about to be cast as the Nurse. They asked us to stay with them in Budapest after visiting Vienna. After dinner, the Professor had intended to take us to his island house, but it was late and we decided it would be fun to see Skansen, the Stockholm folk centre. A Swedish crowd seemed more civilised than an English one. When the evening was over, everyone held hands and sang.

In Uppsala there were hedgehogs on the road and nearby a pond with wild duck.

Recently Yunus sent me a postcard of the town and it didn't look a bit like my memory of it!

A new treatment for one cause of deafness, otosclerosis, was 'in the air'. It's odd the way inventions occur simultaneously in more than one country: the fenestration operation was being developed in many of the places we visited and Oliver brought this technique back to the North of England. Oliver, I suppose, was among the pioneers. Watching and assisting in operations in various parts of the world enabled him to acquire the latest and best methods, and in his turn pass it on to future generations. It was good to work in countries that could afford the most advanced equipment, and also to marvel at the dexterity of surgeons where skill and swiftness were all important to the success of an operation. It was an exciting time in the E.N.T. world and flattering to find crossed Swedish and English flags decorating the tables.

The son of one of our hosts came to stay with us. Anne was still at school so we had to take him with us to grown-up parties. At one, we heard him arguing fiercely with a Brigadier about the date of an English battle. When we got home and looked it up, Klaus proved to be right. He was a good-looking boy. He strode up and down the drawing room, declaiming, 'England is a decadent country. If war is declared, she will lose.' This amused us, but Oliver was disappointed when he offered to buy Klaus a model battleship and he chose two German ones. Yet forty years on, he rang up from Harvard – he, in his turn, a Professor – asking us to stay with him, saying he had never forgotten his visit and its influence on his life!

Anne, when the war was over, stayed with his family. She rang up to ask if she could bring a friend home, remarking casually, 'She is some sort of cousin to the King of Sweden.' I was horrified. 'It's all right,' said Anne, 'she says she will come as a parlour maid.' I had no help whatsoever at that time. A Royal parlour maid would have been the last straw. She didn't come.

Vienna 1938

Oliver believed in reading the literature of the country he was about to visit: Mann, Rilke, Dante, Cervantes. The quotation from Cervantes that was most familiar to Anne and me, because it was often quoted, was 'Hidalgos have no bellies'. Breakfast rolls often had to last us all day. At night there was usually a banquet and there never seemed to be a shortage of champagne.

51

To know one or two psalms by heart, Oliver said, was useful because it was nearly always possible to find a prayer book to act as a crib.

In Sweden, Oliver had acquired letters of introduction to the foremost surgeons in Vienna – they belonged to the generation, that, like Sir St. Clair, counted the 'Crowned Heads of Europe' among their patients. At Victoria Station, posters announced, 'Hitler Invades Austria. Passengers travel at their own risk.' 'Shall we go?' I asked. 'Better, while the going's good,' was his response.

Our first stop was Innsbruck. Sentries guarded the hotel. At dinner, ours was the table without a swastika. We were the only civilians. We joined the throng processing silently along the Maria-Theresien-Strasse. We, and everyone else, looked straight ahead, seeing through the corners of our eyes windows slashed and daubed with tar-black slogans, furniture lying where it had been kicked to pieces by jack-booted feet. No-one dared to stop and stare.

The next day we travelled to Vienna by troop train. At first, the country was mountainous. As it flattened out, we saw from the windows of our carriage an endless stream of armoured cars and tanks. We had no idea the world contained so many. They seemed to go on for ever.

I watched Oliver with some anxiety as he unrolled maps and studied them intently. My instinct that the soldiers were suspicious was confirmed when we arrived in Vienna where we were met by a bearded man speaking faultless English. He escorted us to our taxi, taking careful note that we were staying at Sachers. (Sachers had been chosen because it occurred in a novel that I'd been reading. Sachers, Crowned Heads, E.N.T. men: it all fitted into my picture of Vienna.) The bearded man told us that Hitler had provided soup kitchens – such a good thing for Austria.

Only one of the professors whom we had come to see was still in existence. The others, we were told later, were in a hulk in the middle of the Danube. The remaining one was terrified when we were shown into his consulting room. I had never before witnessed nor experienced the feeling of fear. He shook his head and uttered not one word. He was to join his Jewish colleagues. Men, internationally famous. Does anyone today recall their names?

Oliver worked in operating theatres and clinics with young Nazi surgeons. At eleven o'clock each morning, they trooped outside and sang the Horst Wessel song. At night, they took us to a quiet underground *Weinstube*. We drank Horiger wine, grapes grown in the vineyard of the castle where Richard Lionheart was imprisoned. The wives wore brooches that Oliver admired. They looked like maple leaves, but on closer inspection proved to be maps of the 'New Europe'. The following night they had tactfully discarded them.

It was strange to be drinking and talking to people who were – or who were about to be – our enemies. They said that in every profession, in every business, Jews – once established – kept everyone else out. They were delighted to be at last in possession of the top jobs. We talked of war. Oliver told me later that I kept saying, 'But you can't want to bomb our babies.' They explained that Oliver was in a different category from most English people because he had been in the Navy in the last war. They admired the British Navy.

One night, we dined at the *Drei Hussaren* – very civilised, rather grand. There was a group of black-shirted young officers. Their behaviour was quiet and dignified. It was the expression on every face I shall never forget. I have seen nothing like it before or since, except on War Memorials. When I hear the Shostakovich Seventh Symphony and that ever-recurring melody which becomes more and more sinister, I think of Vienna.

Tanks and armoured cars continued to roll through the city. It seemed absurd to imagine that I was being followed wherever I went. Why on earth should anyone bother to shadow me? Yet we were both watched.

We decided not to continue our journey through to Budapest. We heard later that the Hungarian E.N.T. man whom we had met with his charming wife in Sweden and who had given us introductions to the Viennese professors had committed suicide.

We had travelled to Vienna with soldiers released from Schuschnigg's concentration camp. This time, our companions were a middle-aged Jewish man and wife: they were at the far end of the compartment. Fear is a miasma that we were beginning to recognise. We arrived at the frontier in the middle of the night. Doors were flung open, and in the *wagon lits* next to ours there were dreadful sounds – difficult to describe, sounds never before heard. Four armed jack-booted Nazis were not inclined to listen to Oliver at first; thank heaven for his imperturbability and fairly fluent German. It took time to make them look at our passports and understand that they had no cause to deal with us as they had with the poor Austrians. They, I think, knew that they would never reach safety.

We stayed at Aylesbury on our way home. The local cricket club was celebrating – clanking their beer tankards and singing their own version of 'The Lincolnshire Poacher'. Never a sign of a soldier, a tank, a gun carriage. Did England know? Peace can be frightening.

Once I locked everything I had written away in a drawer. Now I let Jane read and comment. She was in Tibet last year, doctor to an expedition of seven professional women following in the footsteps of Alexandra David-Neel. The film they brought back premièred in Paris in the presence of the Dalai Lama. Jane gave him a letter concerning aid to Tibetan refugees from Médecins du Monde, the humanitarian organisation for which she works.

Back to Jane's comments. She is concerned lest her grandmama had Nazi tendencies in her youth. She was horrified that in Vienna, knowing that the Jewish professors we had gone specially to meet were in hulks on the Danube (so we were told), we, instead of going straight home, writing to the newspapers and telling the world, stayed and hob-nobbed with their successors. It never occurred to us to do otherwise. It was a strange time. We were in a kind of limbo.

Children of three now are more aware of the reality of horror and violence than we were in those days. Hannah, our great-grandchild, seeing a policeman in an English shop, wanted to run and hide, or else shoot him. She had known a child who was shot by a policeman in Pietermaritzburg.

It was at this moment, thinking how the young travel today, that a spot of time leapt to my mind: it was the only time I was ever in London alone. I must have been about twenty, staying with an aunt. Oliver came to meet me at Victoria Station. 'This seems to be the conventional form of greeting,' he said as he bent to kiss me. Mother had told me, 'Never allow a man to kiss you unless you are engaged to be married to him.' I resisted. He persisted. I ran. It occurred to me as I ran with Oliver in pursuit that no-one appeared to take the slightest notice, even when I climbed the ladder. It was a tall ladder – the roof was being painted or repaired. I can't remember how we got down and whether he kissed me in the end. But I can still picture those acres of girders and glass roof. Here is a poem of Oliver's: he too must have remembered the incident – only he made the station Waterloo, to rhyme with taboo! (It *was* Victoria.)

TO SHEONA

The revelation adumbrates light that transcends our own,
To set aglow the pearly gates that rest on precious stone
As rare as lapis or as jade, that seems from heaven sent:
So is the gaze I serenade, so wise and innocent.

If inner light be best revealed by Saint John the Divine,
Light veins of ore remain concealed in inspiration's mine.
No herds or flocks for dowry your father left, but skill
To cast your winged and hackled fly: full on the hook ran Will.
Against your charms I was not proof, but kisses were taboo:
You climbed a ladder to the roof; was that at Waterloo?
Enabled to express your views in prose precise and terse,
You eloquently wake the muse in elevated verse.
More piquant were a pasquinade, could I lampoon some fault,
But such perfection to upbraid would brand me as a dolt.
When overseas, *sin embargo*, there'd never be a war,
If one so *muy simpatico* were Queen's ambassador.
With genes in trust to propagate, of candles we lit five,
The flame of hope to generate: in light may they survive.
Your care my life so often saves, My Compass and My Chart.
O Thou who walkest on the waves, watch over my sweetheart!

Before the Second World War, we still thought that the seas performed 'their task of pure ablution round earth's human shores'; the rivers ran sweet, teeming with trout and salmon – although Father was concerned about the effect of industrial waste at the mouth of the river Tees. We each had our individual joys and tragedies, but for us, and for the masses all over the world, there seemed to be hope. The happy ending was expected – as in *Pilgrim's Progress* – when one got to the river. On the other side there would be no money, no politics, no problems. Yet – could there be happiness in heaven if on earth there was so much sadness?

The Thanksgiving Day party had seemed such a good idea. Laurence had married a pretty American wife. It was a lovely evening. We were in the garden. The Territorials were going to fire the two cannons captured at Waterloo. The cannons went off with a little 'pop' and we all laughed. They stuffed in some more gunpowder, or whatever it was. This time there was quite a bang. The girl next to me fell over my feet. 'I think she's fainted,' I said to Oliver. He bent down. 'She's dead. Stay beside her: don't leave her,' he told me and rushed to the Colonel who lay, his inside lying outside on the ground beside him. Oliver went with him in the ambulance; he survived. The husband of the dead girl knelt over her, sobbing. It seemed suddenly to have turned dark. They'd just had their first baby. It was the last party before the Second World War ...

Chapter Five

WAR AND AFTER

Oliver thought that, having held in the last war commissions in both the Army and the Navy, this time he would choose the Air Force.

I thought of Chera, Oliver's mother, in the Great War, proud of her husband and sons: Durham in Mesopotamia, Oliver at sea, Edmund in France, their father in the R.A.M.C. – too old for active service, but in uniform. In the Second World War, people didn't regard a man in mufti as a coward and hand him a white feather.

My fear was of Oliver wanting to be a hero. Thank goodness he was told he was needed in operating theatres at home. The wards were soon full of wounded.

Petrol was rationed, so Oliver got a motor bike, keeping the car for London meetings. The happy recollection I have of the war is of empty roads. Signposts had been removed. One night in early summer, we lost our way and meandered through lanes white with May. We had no idea where we were – just somewhere in the middle of England as it might have been centuries ago.

Our first experience of the Blitz was when we were staying at the Langham. We'd travelled all night; Oliver had shaved, washed and gone to a meeting, leaving me wallowing in my bath. The siren sounded and I dressed pretty quickly and decided that it was safer to walk down stairs instead of taking the lift. I expected to see people hastening to an air raid shelter. In fact, they were sitting quietly, reading their morning papers. I descended the last few stairs in as calm and dignified a manner as I could muster, chose a comfortable chair and opened my *Times*. Glancing down, I realised that, though below the waist I was fully clad, above I was wearing merely a bra. Later the Langham had a direct hit and was totally destroyed.

The Second World War began with gas masks, black-out and sirens. Green Leas had many windows and an enormous skylight, surrounded by a waist-high wooden parapet that each evening had to have lengths of plywood lowered over it by ropes.

After Dunkirk, we were asked to take billetees. The first subaltern fell in love with Oliver's secretary; when he came home from India they married, so that was a happy ending. The next took us to see *Maid of the Mountains*, which he thought simply wonderful. I wish he'd had someone young to share his delight, but perhaps it was as well there wasn't. He was killed.

When the time came for them to go, it was supposed to be kept a secret, but of course it couldn't be when we were in the same house, so we always took them to the station. Halifax station at 5.45 a.m. on a cold November morning is the most desolate place you can imagine. We were not allowed onto the platform. It wasn't quite as bad as it would have been had they been sons, but very nearly.

A Captain asked if we'd let his wife come and stay. They were both County tennis players. They were grateful to us for letting them be together, and were sweet to Fiona. Our tennis improved wonderfully. They were less dependent on our cooking, which was a relief. I don't think we were expected to feed them all, but of course we did. It was at a tennis party that the news came that Paddy Nugent, who was in the Tank Regiment, had been killed. He was older than Anne, who was still at school, but he was one of our friends.

The shrapnel that splattered on our wardens' helmets was mostly from our own batteries. The Germans were concentrating on Liverpool. Halifax was only once badly bombed.

Leaving London after a particularly alarming air raid, we decided we would take Anne home to comparative safety. When we arrived at her School House, it was in complete darkness and there was an eerie silence, broken by an ear-splitting yell. Lights went on; they had been playing a game of Murder. Until the Americans commandeered Wycombe Abbey, she remained at school. Her first M.B. exam at South Kensington was taken partly under a table with flying bombs overhead.

One Christmas dinner was a skimpy and elderly oxtail.

After Oliver had been operating at Northallerton, we called at a farm to see if we could buy eggs. There was a most delicious smell of roast duck issuing from the kitchen. The farmer's wife said she could let us have half-a-dozen eggs and she was sorry there was no butter, but the policeman had just been and bought the lot. We guessed he was also having supper with them and the thought of sage and onions, duck and apple sauce remained with us for ages.

Oliver was offered a post in Bath that sounded lovely. Very Jane Austenish: we were promised a party in the Assembly Rooms to welcome us – a string band, palms around the platform and a Duchess! – consulting rooms in the Crescent and a flat in the house that had been Sickert's. Oliver's wards in Yorkshire were full of soldiers and he felt he couldn't leave them. I still have the letters from Bath. The Green Leas kitchen sometimes seemed like an extension of the Officers'

Mess. One evening I remember seeing it filled with officers eating fish and chips. I went out briefly and came back to an empty room. Reports of Hitler's Invasion had reached us.

Halifax was the headquarters of the Duke of Wellington's Regiment. Perhaps we all felt a little reflected glory when the current Duke was stationed in our midst. He was a subaltern and didn't look like the descendent of the victor of Waterloo. Everyone who knew him well said that he was awfully nice. However, when the Regiment disembarked at Salerno and the sergeant took everyone's name, it was probably not surprising that he thought this young man was pulling his leg. He was killed, and his uncle inherited the title.

I've said practically nothing about the Second World War and now I am remembering Waterloo. Granny's great-aunt prepared each night for escape should Boney land at the mouth of the Tyne. War was a horrid, miserable time.

At this moment, Amstrad flashed:

FATAL

I ring Rick. 'It's not as bad as it sounds,' he said. 'It doesn't mean what you think it means.'

POST-WAR CONFERENCES

Chicago 1947

In 1947, Oliver became a Founder Fellow of the International College of Surgeons and was invited to be a guest speaker in Chicago for the E.N.T. section. A second cable came asking if he would also address the full College on a subject of general interest. He chose to talk about 'handedness'. He had trained himself to be ambidextrous, because it enhanced his operating skill.

This theme led us to spirals: shells, climbing plants, corkscrews in mid-ocean (there, even I was baffled) and the twists of retinal blood vessels of tylopods, which took us to London Zoo. There are peculiarities in the comparative anatomy of the eye in the Family Tylopoda: camels, llamas, vicuñas (incidentally, tylopods are even-toed ruminants).

Incipient twists are sometimes discernible in the human retina –

Which is why
Armed with an
Ophthalmoscope
We went to the Zoo
In the hope
Of looking into
The eye of a
Tylopod.

Camels spit
Llamas are haughty.

On the Mappin Terrace
A vicuña
From Ecuador,
Never handled before,
Seeing the ophthalmoscope
Fled to me
Hiding her head in my coat.

You may think
What I say silly,
You may consider
'God' merely a rhyme
For Tylopod.

The truth is
The trust of
A timid
Vicuña
Induces
Emotional
Overtones
Scientists
Do not attempt to explain.

We also visited the Reptile House. The crocodile nursery is a fascinating place – babies of all ages and sizes. The keeper held in his arms a fairly small one, while Oliver examined its throat. A crocodile has a continuous passage from nostril to windpipe which enables it to drown its prey while breathing itself. It also has a tail that can give a well-wisher an almighty swipe. Oliver was gentle with it. He had gentle and 'feeling' hands. To me, even the most juvenile crocodile appeared sinister.

Hearing a commotion in the corridor, I went to see what was happening. I saw a middle-aged woman with peroxided hair and fingers glistening with diamonds, kneeling beside a live and very large crocodile incarcerated in a kind of coffin – she was kissing its snout. Dogs show affection, cats ecstasy, and this crocodile – I can still hardly believe it – did really appear to demonstrate fondness. How can one recognise any kind of emotion, other than appetite, in one of the few survivors whose fossil ancestors can be traced back to the times of the Dinosaurs? But there was absolutely no doubt – it was pleased to see her. 'I'm back, my pet. You are coming home,' she murmured, and off they went, the crocodile in its coffin carried by several keepers, the peroxide woman at its side.

'What on earth …' I said to the Head Keeper. 'Don't ask me,' he said. 'We've none of us seen anything like it. She's a fortune teller. She brings it here when she has to go away. We dare not touch the brute.' 'Is it doped?' I asked. 'No,' he said. 'It just responds.'

Sheona and Oliver after the Second World War

Now we were ready for Chicago. In the early post-war years, we were still rationed, and travel a problem. Only because we knew someone 'in the Canadian Pacific' – he had been stationed with the Royal Engineers in Halifax – were we able to get to America.

Liverpool docks had always been magic. I'd been taken to see a wonderful liner in 1909. Now I was to sail in one! We stood – a group of us – gazing up at the *Empress of Canada*. 'Do you always travel by this line?' I asked the little lady next to me, the enormous bouquet she had been presented with failing to conceal the fact she was pregnant. 'I *am* the Canadian Pacific,' she replied.

I was seasick from the mouth of the Mersey to the mouth of the St. Lawrence.

We had a week in Toronto, Oliver working in hospitals and the museum. We were taken to Niagara 'just for a run in the evening'. Oliver took a photograph of me with my back to the Falls, listening intently to a woman professor's story of her proposal of marriage the previous week. She could not decide whether to marry the man. 'They always bring us here to propose,' she said. The Falls must have been magnificent before they were surrounded by concrete. It would have been nice to go up-stream.

In the train on the way to Chicago, a young man asked me if I was English, and if he could talk to me. He was of German origin and the war for him had been awful. He had been in the U.S. Air Force, dropping bombs on his own people.

I met several mothers whose sons had been killed 'fighting for someone else's country'.

When we arrived at the Palmer House, where we were staying in Chicago, Oliver was besieged by reporters. I heard him trying to explain to them that in England doctors could be struck off the register for any talk that would sound like advertising. The only other Englishman was Sir Zachary Cope. He and Oliver made speeches at one of the banquets. Sir Zachary composed his on the back of his menu in verse, talking to me at the same time.

Lake Shore Drive was surprisingly beautiful. White skyscrapers against a blue sky and white waves breaking on the shore.

Going to church in Chicago was quite an experience. Imagine an opera house half way up a skyscraper, with rest rooms, a library, a study and flood lighting. The service was unexpectedly moving. When the Canadian Pacific Railway was under construction, men met in a hut to sing hymns. From this beginning, the church had grown.

I saw only the best bits of Chicago: the Field Museum, the Art Gallery and one drive into the country. We hurtled through an Arboretum at what seemed to be one hundred miles an hour, so we couldn't see the trees. It was dangerous to pause, they said, because gangsters were liable to pounce upon one with revolvers. A strange city where Indian names and legends still persist.

Oliver had invented a machine that recorded the patient's heartbeat when on the operating table. A man in Chicago had had the same idea and Oliver went to see him. He offered to test Oliver's heart and found it behaving in a peculiar manner. Oliver said this was not surprising, since two bullets had gone whistling past his ear. 'Oh,' said the man, 'That's just cops and bums.'

The hospitals had all the latest equipment and instruments, and the offer of a post in one of them was really rather tempting, but we didn't think that Fiona would flourish in the States. Americans were extraordinarily kind and hospitable. Friends we made there came to see us in England. They said Oliver did more operations in a morning than they did in a week.

When we went to pay our hotel bill, we discovered we really were 'guests', which was fortunate because, when we rejoined our ship in Quebec, we hadn't a cent in our pockets. We hadn't even money to buy a pair of nylon stockings. Nylons hadn't yet appeared in England.

Rome 1948

We went to Rome in 1948. I remember my amazement, when leaving the airfield, to find that we were driving along the Appian Way, past the Colosseum and the Forum. I remember the Forum, empty except for an old man cutting the grass, with a donkey at his side, and Oliver standing on an altar, practising his talk in Italian; swifts screaming overhead.

'Remember,' said Pope Pius XII, 'every patient should be as dear to you as parent or child.' We were nearly late for the Audience because Oliver was working until the last minute and we had to buy a square of black lace for me to wear on my head. Fortunately, there was a shop near the Vatican. We sped, panting, past the Swiss Guard, to arrive just in time.

The party at the Villa d'Este was a midsummer dream. Wives and daughters of Roman surgeons dressed in medieval clothes greeted us in the amphitheatre beneath a waterfall, dark and mysterious after the sunlit terraces and sparkling fountains.

Why should I remember – knowing no Italian – the name *Nubofragia Violentissimo*? I can't even spell it. Never have I known such thunder and lightning. We were in evening dress after a *Concerto di Danze* at the University. A young Russian gallantly gave us his taxi and strode away into the storm. Had he only one dinner jacket? Would it be ruined? I have liked Russians ever since.

Our *pensione* had been chosen for us by the Foreign Office. When we set off for the opera, all the Italian maids gathered round and admired my dress.

One awful confession: we never saw the Sistine Chapel, though we did kiss the toe of St. Peter.

This letter from a Fellow of the College illustrates how important the British Government felt these meetings to be:

London W.1
4th April, 1948

Dear Mr. Lodge,

International College of Surgeons.
Meeting in Rome, 18th to 23rd May, 1948

Not only are the arrangements regarding holding the meeting in statu quo, but a political position has arisen which makes the holding of this meeting of more than surgical importance, as the enclosed copy of a letter from the Foreign Office demonstrates. It is most important that the meeting should be well-attended by British surgeons, and I would be very glad to get your confirmation that you will attend as originally arranged.

The Foreign Office has been in touch with the Bank of England, who state that an adequate grant will be made.

With kind regards,
Yours sincerely,
Hamilton Bailey.

Venice 1950

In 1950 we went to Venice. The Aga Khan and Rita Hayworth arrived at the Danielli just as we did. As she stepped out of their gondola, the film star's sable cape slipped from her shoulders and fell with a splash into the canal. Porters rushed forward to try and fish it out. She waved them aside. 'It was of no importance,' she said.

When we went into the dining room, the head waiter welcomed Oliver with outstretched arms imagining him to be the manager of the Savoy. Mistaken identity probably accounted for our magnificent bedroom with a balcony overlooking the Grand Canal.

An American woman spent a lot of her time on the adjoining balcony and when Oliver was working I heard her life story. She had been married to a man who was immensely rich. He used to wake her up in the middle of the night saying, 'Honey I have an urge for chop suey. The only place for decent chop suey is San Francisco,' and he would haul her out of bed into their private plane. She got tired of this and divorced him. Now she was married to an older and even richer man. He too was tiresome. He was taking her round the world, staying in the most exclusive hotels and all she wanted to do was to get home to her dogs. She thought that if the folk in Venice had any sense they would fill the canals with concrete. She wrote to me for years ('Dear gracious, charming, lovely Sheona …') telling me all about her dogs and the famous film producers with whom she stayed.

We had been to Torcello (where Oliver made a speech after dinner), we had been to the Teatro La Fenice – the play in Italian – we'd been taken on a tour of the churches by the particularly nice wife of a surgeon and had coffee with a friend of hers in a palazzo on the Grand Canal. Marble floors and rather empty: one guessed that she'd had to sell beautiful furniture and jewellery in order to go on living there. We'd seen the Doge's Palace and sat at a table in the Piazza San Marco listening to one string orchestra after another. We'd had lunch with delightful Americans in a wistaria-covered restaurant. The first time I'd tasted scampi. We'd been to a glass factory and watched Americans choosing what seemed to us the less attractive pieces.

I shall always regret that I did not go to Padua to listen to Oliver's talk at the University: I had simply run out of energy. Instead I sat in St Mark's. It was dark and quiet, as if it held the whole of history. Little groups were following priests in monk-like robes. Italian parents were there with their children gathering serenity. I couldn't describe a single feature of St Mark's. It is odd that I remember that hour…

Buenos Aires 1950

I didn't go with Oliver to Buenos Aires in 1950. We were still only allowed to take a small amount of money out of the country. Oliver had a long talk with Eva Perón. He could not help finding her charming. She told him that she was dying and was really interested in the hospital.

More hob-nobbing with dictators. Oh dear!

Florence 1951

The congress in Florence the following year opened at the Palazzo Vecchio. On either side of the platform stood soldiers of the Florentine Guard in their medieval uniform of scarlet, with stockings cross-gartered, pointed shoes and flat pancake bonnets. We were greeted with a fanfare of trumpets.

Each day there were papers to be read, operations to be watched by the surgeons. For the wives, every moment was occupied. The first day, there was a dress show. An American woman said, 'Life is the same the world over. This is what we do at home, sit and drink and watch mannequin parades.' It seemed far removed from the life some of us led.

We hurried back to our hotel to dress for a ball at the Pitti Palace to be held in the White Salon, never seen by the general public. Princess Margaret and Princess Elizabeth danced there. Florence is renowned for the grace, charm and culture of its women. Whenever I saw Oliver, he was dancing with girls who looked as if they'd stepped out of a Botticelli frame. He assured me on each occasion he was only having an Italian lesson.

I found myself drifting from one period of history to another: Renaissance when talking to Italians; then, with Americans, the dream faded and one was very much in the present. Italian women never drink spirits but, as I was with a group of Americans, I accepted a glass of whisky and said apologetically, 'The English need a good strong drink to make them human.' This so exactly voiced their opinion of us that they roared with laughter and wrote it down in their note books. We left the Pitti Palace at 3.00 a.m. The fountains were playing, the streets were silent except for the clatter of our horses' hooves over the cobbles.

We had to be up early the next morning; Oliver to work, Anne and I to join the rest of our gathering at the Uffizi. The only pictures I remember are the Botticellis and Filippo Lippi's *Madonna*. Next, a drive to Fiesole. We strolled among olive trees and poppies through the ruins of a Roman theatre and baths recently excavated. While we were there, Oliver was reading his paper in Italian.

I arrived at the banquet exhausted. To dance until three and sight-see from nine to seven was strenuous. Anne discovered her place-card next to a handsome German, who said he was sorry he had not been more polite when they met at Fiesole, but he'd imagined she must be American. Since she was English, that was another story. Surrounded by young German and Italian doctors, she had a lively evening.

I searched for my place in vain, but found an empty chair next to a nice American surgeon. We were finishing the first course when I heard a gentle voice saying, 'If you will forgive me, Signora, you are supposed to be sitting next to me.' I followed him all the way up the room, conscious of a sudden silence and every woman's eye examining my outfit. We had agreed in the afternoon to ignore instructions on the invitation and wear cocktail dresses, because the American women couldn't wear the dresses they'd worn for the ball the previous night, and were keeping their others for Paris. My cocktail dress was in a very different category from theirs. In England, we still had to produce coupons for clothes.

It was the President of the conference that I followed to the top table and found that he was on my right, the Mayor on my left. The Mayor and I discovered that our common language was French and we neither of us understood one word that the other uttered. He was extremely polite and, at appropriate intervals, we turned and beamed upon each other and he pressed a carnation into my hand. Soon the flowers that littered his end of the table were piled in front of me.

The President, who professed to speak no English, became fluent. He was charming, widely read, an admirer of Mr. Churchill, so, although I was too agitated to eat, the evening flew. He told me that Oliver's paper had been excellent and that he'd been impressed by his knowledge of Leopardi and Dante. Next came the speeches. The interpreter told me that Oliver's – in Italian – contained the most delightful and original thoughts. Why was I invited to sit in the place of honour? Since the American President's wife was absent, I may have been a safe substitute as an outsider.

I forgot to tell Jane that the Mayor – who really was charming – happened to be a communist!

Madrid 1952

In 1952 Anne came with us to Madrid. Oliver knew *Don Quixote* backwards. He was delighted to see the 'Monumento a Cervantes' in the Plaza de España. As I have said, Anne and I became resigned to being told that 'Hidalgos have no bellies'.

In Toledo, we saw the marvellous El Grecos, and witnessed a bullfight. At the bullfight, a Harley Street surgeon, looking very British in bowler hat and carrying a rolled umbrella, remarked when I asked if he'd enjoyed the performance, 'Oh, good show! Good show!' The following day he passed us as we were standing disconsolately beside a friend's car, with its windows broken and a precious camera stolen. 'Bad show! Bad show!' he murmured, slightly quickening his stride.

The famous Manolete was killed recently in a bullfight. Dane Chandos says, 'the life of a bullfighter is the quintessence of life in Spain today, without the hunger. There is colour and glitter and drama, there is pride and grace and bravery, there is exaltation and there is bitterness. But behind it all, at the back of every Torero's or every Spaniard's mind, is the ever-present question of what tomorrow may bring, and just as the past has been filled with sorrow and with pain and with death, so must the future appear misted over with shadows and dark with forebodings of violence and ruin.'

The procession in strict order – Matadors with their team of Banderilleros, Picadors mounted carrying their pikes, Monos with mules who drag dead bulls from the arena. The Duke of Prima de Rivera, who had been Spanish Ambassador in London, had ordained that horses should be padded.

From Toledo, we arrived in the evening at a castella some miles away, to find tables spread with fine linen and glittering silver and our hosts distraught because an uninvited horde had descended upon them and demolished the food. We wondered if General Franco's daughter, who with us was watching Flamenco dancing, was as hungry as we were.

At midnight, dancing over, we went to rejoin our luxurious bus. It had gone. We tried to board another – it was full. Abandoned in what appeared to be a dark forest, surrounded by a herd of fighting bulls, we had a moment of panic. Only the performers' bus was left. Oliver managed to prise open the safety exit door and we crouched behind the dancers. It was an ancient bus with no springs. We'd had two rolls for breakfast and nothing since. Anne and I were not Hidalgos. It seemed a long way to Madrid.

A postcard from Anne to Oliver's secretary says of General Franco's daughter, 'She is young, beautiful and gracious. In my shaky French, I told her how impressed I have been by the speed of Spanish surgeons. They are as quick and dexterous as the Toreador. The bullfight was just like this picture.'

Jane is horrified.

At a banquet the following night, Anne and I were presented with fans. I still have mine to prove that memories of Spain are not all fantasy.

The Prado was a magnificent setting for another party, but left little time to look at the pictures. No-one could fail to see the *Little Infanta*. Oliver kept in his dressing room a print of Ribera's *Jacob's Dream*, with angels ascending and descending the ladder.

All this and I've said nothing about General Franco's dramatic appearance at the University. Sitting in an open limousine, surrounded by armed motor cyclists, he roared up to the steps, escorted by Generals and Admirals in magnificent uniforms and medals galore.

The Duke of Prima de Rivera's widow, Pila Primode y Saenzde, asked me to meet her to talk about the role of women in Spain. I had the choice of discovering a great deal from her, or of merely setting eyes on General Franco. I think I made the wrong decision.

Holland 1953

We went to Holland immediately after the Coronation. This is part of the letter I wrote to Aunt Madge:

> We were off to Holland before we had time fully to digest the coronation. We found everyone overflowing with enthusiasm and admiration for Elizabeth II. Dutch boys collect her photograph, their fathers blow an appreciative kiss when her name is mentioned. The Americans say that in her they see hope for the world. Everyone flocking to see the film. It is a little hard on the stars, having Royal competition! It can't be merely that we see her through rosy spectacles, because on every side one heard praise for her charm and beauty. Certainly her every movement and gesture is regal, and yet she appears perfectly simple and natural.
>
> It was fun going with Mary and Michael Stewart to Westminster in the special train. The underground thronged with peers in coronets at 6.00 a.m. and placards announcing the conquest of Everest. Mary looked so nice in her coffee-coloured lace dress and the veil she had to wear in the Abbey.
>
> We had an excellent view from our stand under Big Ben, in the pouring rain, and we enjoyed luncheon on the terrace of the House. We sat next to a nice man and his wife. The only clue we had to their identity was that he was the grandson of the oldest peer. Later I was offered a share of the most holey umbrella I have ever seen by Lady Davidson's sister.
>
> In the evening we drove with Mary and her friend Molly Hob-

man to look at the fireworks, and we enjoyed that very much too. When people envy me for my opportunities for foreign travel, I think it is really because they think I don't deserve it! No-one would envy Mary for that reason. Although Michael's position may be partly responsible for the interesting life she leads, it is chiefly due to her own character and intelligence. There is lots to be learned from both of them. It's good to combine love of the arts with devotion to public duty!

Our departure for Holland was not as calm and orderly as one would have wished. We had arranged to leave for Hull at 5.30 p.m. At 5.40, Anne discovered that she could not get into either of her evening dresses which she had washed herself. As Oliver arrived from the Infirmary, ready to leave, he met Anne and me setting off for the shops, which were just about to close. By a stroke of good luck, we found a dress which both fitted and suited her. It isn't easy to have suitable clothes for all occasions when there is either a reception, an excursion or a banquet each day. Anne always looked just right.

Prince Bernhard represented Queen Juliana at the opening ceremony. He spoke excellent English and we all felt very endeared to him because we thought he was rather like Prince Philip, only less glamorous. Certainly he was both charming and intelligent.

There were delegates from thirty-nine nations. Oliver found the papers and films of the utmost interest – and his own went well. It was nice for Anne to meet Professor Döhlman and his wife again. You remember she stayed with them in Sweden.

A charming Swiss woman told me she met Anne on an expedition to Delft and the Hague, organised, in theory, by the Ladies' Committee; in practice, by Anne. My informant dissolved into helpless laughter when she described Anne taking charge, and everyone, even the Dutch hostess, following her blindly. Anyway, she must have been impressed as well as amused, as she invited us all, including Fiona, to stay.

At the banquet I sat next to a Hindu from Bombay and discovered the necessity for contemplation. It is vital to get in tune with the infinite in this life, and one should embrace trouble and sorrow as a means to this end. The thing I like best about his religion is the belief that anyone can reach the state of Nirvana, be he Jew or Christian or what you will. I can't say I like the idea of the transmigration of souls. Let us hope that in this respect they are mistaken!

Oliver had a lovely time with all the Spanish ladies who are too beautiful and enchanting for words. They are like humming birds or tropical butterflies, rather than mere mammals! The husbands are at first suspicious and quite prepared to fight a duel – then they too fall under his spell and before we know where we are, we are all being invited to Valencia or Brazil.

On our way home I thought, here at last is a journey without adventure. Usually where Oliver goes, avalanches occur, planes make forced landings, passports disappear and dictators take possession. We went on deck. There was thick fog and the sea was glassy. All the other passengers stayed below. The look-out man called at intervals, 'Ship on the starboard bow.' We stood silent, gazing into nothingness and listening intently for any sound. A volley of screams from our siren, very near to us an answering hoot, and out of the fog loomed a craft about our own size. Our skipper yelled, 'Full speed astern!' and then the incredible happened. Like a film when the express train comes straight for you. The other ship was apparently intent upon a head-on collision. At the last minute, it shot across our bows with an inch to spare and we rammed each other sideways. A calm sea and a spice of danger are infinitely preferable to a rough crossing.

This chapter is about foreign travel. My sister Mary Stewart had told me that I was neglecting my responsibilities to the community, so between conferences, I became a governor of three secondary modern schools, Vice Chairman of a Literary and Philosophical Society, President of a Townswomen's Guild and was on one of the committees of the Council of Social Services. What was much more fun was a writing class at a technical school. That's why the War Chapter is so short.

I'm a bit like a sundial that only recalls the sunny hours, and I tend to forget the anxious ones. Oliver had an operation which was a nightmare, and I had two major ones myself. No longer were there skating parties in lovely gardens with supper afterwards. As I try to remember those days, bits of sadness crop up and I find myself drawing a curtain across them.

Retirement brought a new lease of life.

Chapter Six

RETIREMENT AND WRITING

WRAYSHOLME

We'd sought it here, we'd sought it there
From the Isle of Man to a place near Ware:
When agents mentioned a price we'd say,
'We'll think about it,' and walk away:
We told each other we mustn't be rash,
Nobody pays for a dream in cash.

Some had dry rot and sagging thatch,
Doors and windows that would not latch.
O. rather fancied a Border keep
With a *garde-de-lieu*, and going cheap.
The moat, rank with nettles and old tin cans,
He peopled with water lilies and swans.

F. made no comment, how could she say,
'The only solution is simply to pray';
This she did to some purpose and so
She found us the perfect house, and lo
And behold, our dream came true –
A garden, a balcony – and a view!

So – here we are, retired in Ambleside. Windows overlooking Loughrigg and Fairfield (my private fantasy is to blast a hole through Loughrigg in order to see the Langdales!). The lawn would become a forest of oaks if we didn't cut the grass. Fiona's labrador, Spruce, dug up a couple of arrow heads in the garden. A redwood tree had been planted by the former owners, cherished by the man of the house, regarded with anxiety by the wife. Anne says, 'The Redwood stands for Father, the house is Mother.'

Oliver regretted that, after an operation from which he thought he'd never recover, he had decided to resign from the Yorkshire Flyfishers. The rivers Eden and Eamont were now temptingly near. However, there was still our Beck in Yorkshire.

One never ceases to marvel at coincidences. Oliver had been asked to become a governor of Skellfield, now a direct grant-school removed to a stately home and flourishing. No-one had the least idea that I had been a former pupil. Skellfield was not far from the Beck!

After a function at which the Archbishop of York had presided, we repaired to our old haunts, shedding our glad rags for fishing togs beside the bridge I'd known all my days.

Oliver began to concentrate on music. He hadn't had a lesson since he was ten. He now played the organ every Sunday at Holy Trinity, Brathay. His maestros, Mr. Lewis and Roger Fiske, were amused and patient. I dreaded to hear, 'You can't play that, it's far too difficult.' I knew the congregation would suffer. I did. He also began to paint. A renowned artist has assured me that by the year 2091 his pictures will have been 'discovered'.

Fiona, by finding Wraysholme, had launched us in to another world.

As a little girl, my mind seethed with stories, too wonderful to keep to myself. Alas, on paper they turned to ash. If only I had listened to Humpty Dumpty in *Alice* and discovered how to manipulate words. Why should a thrush sing and a sparrow merely chirp? Throughout my adult years, I had written poems and torn them up.

A simple question from Sue, aged four, led to a train of events which changed my life. Angus and Jane were with Oliver, who was

Wraysholme

fishing. Sue and I wandered along the lane. We were to meet the others at the bridge. 'Tell me about great-grandfather,' she said. In less than three minutes, she ran off to gather blackberries. How boring can one be! When we got home, I wrote a poem and put it away in a drawer.

THEIR GREAT-GRANDFATHER

What was he like? the children ask.
The Beck, so secret overgrown
By willow, alder, does it bask
Beneath June roses, still unknown?

A tapered cast; spliced greenheart rod,
A Greenwell's Glory, Dun, March Brown;
The corner pool where cows have trod
Flies falling light as thistledown.

October! Unpolluted Tees,
The Stag pool favoured salmon run,
Selecting flies beneath chrome trees
Jock Scott or Silver Wilkinson.

Donside in April and its banks ablaze
With broom – 'it fishes best when broom is out'
He said. Oyster-catchers, we seldom found
Their nests! Sandpipers, redshanks, curlews, larks,
Their cries all mingle with the caw of rooks
Above the Rookery stream, and anxious sheep
Recalling lambs who've strayed; they make the air
Vibrate with sound. Above Keig Bridge we go –
Past cherry and white lilac – lizards dart.
At last we reach Broom Brae, put up our rods
Select a Baigent's Brown – one eye upon
The stone of curious shape, it's there a trout
Of quite phenomenal size is sure to lurk.
Bright sun, strong wind, a normal fishing day.
The river ripples round our feet; Broom Brae
Is beautiful, but just a pool, no more.

And then there comes a hatch of fly, greentail
Or grannom, for their eggs are emerald
Green, smooth, velvet, in clouds they come upstream
Engulfing every bush; the females dip
So lightly on the whirling eddying
Miniature waves that swirl behind each stone:
Head, tail, they rise, the tense and and urgent trout,
Or with a merest dimple suck the fly.
Seen from the bank it may not seem like this,
But in the transformed pool a miracle's
Occurred; the strength, the vital quivering force
In every dorsal fin and Y-shaped tail.
For once we're seeing not as stranger sees,
But as a trout.

A few weeks later, this letter arrived:

You may remember me from E.N.T. days! But this is about fishing
… My friend, Frank Elder, has written to me and I enclose his
letter … Please give my best wishes to Oliver. I hope he is en-
joying his retirement.

The enclosed letter began:

Dear Tom,
After we got back from the Don in May, Joan told me that you
knew the whereabouts of Dr. Baigent's daughter.

This led to a visit from Frank Elder and his wife, Joan. I hadn't real-
ised how famous Father had become. I showed Frank my poem. He
asked if he could keep it. A few days later came a letter from David
Colquhoun, the Editor of *The Journal of The Flyfishers' Club*:

If you could manage some reminiscences about your Father, I
should be most flattered and grateful … I must congratulate you
upon your poem.

What had Sue started? From then on, the arrival of the post was the
event of the day. What is more, there came letters from the U.S.A.
leading to the publication of poems and articles and, even better,
lasting friendships. Those were the heady days. 'Who was that ring-

ing up?' Oliver or Fiona would ask. 'Just a call from America,' I'd reply airily, or 'Only a couple of editors from London.' Many of them came to stay. I was asked to the Flyfishers' Club, a strictly male establishment; at luncheon, I should have met men who knew my father. Why did I never go?

Letters ended, 'with love'. What did Oliver think? It seems to me that everyone is searching for someone it is 'safe' to be fond of. A grandmother exactly fills this bill. A restful role that hurts no-one. It was fun for me, and interesting for Oliver because the Editors were delightful, clever and utterly charming men.

So here is the first piece I wrote.

WILLIAM BAIGENT, M.D.

'Think like a trout,' he said. No problem for a five-year-old. As we slid into the stream beside the willow we entered the world of the trout, otter and kingfisher. There was teeming life too beneath each stone. He explained how larvae grew active as they approached maturity, how the nymph left the shelter of the stone to undergo change to winged existence as a fly; how it rose with undulating movement against the current, rested below the surface; the outer cover fractured, and with a wriggling movement the fly emerged from its case.

'It's during this rise,' he writes in his notes, 'that fish are eagerly searching for food. The artificial fly need not be, and will kill no better for being an exact copy, but should bear a resemblance to the nymph in active movement.'

The Beck was so overgrown that it could only be fished upstream, with a flick of the wrist, using sometimes the right hand, sometimes the left. Whether fishing wet, or dry, he was speculating on how the fly appeared to the fish. What were the effects of refraction and interference? Was the trout partially colour blind – a buoyant fly silhouetted, or the sparkle of its hackle seen?

Noticing trout rising splashily, we'd look on the gravel bed. Frail flies with long spidery legs can be seen running about in hundreds, the smaller males in pursuit of the females, on gusty days in April or May. These were caught by the wind and blown over the surface of the water, often across or against the current. 'It affects the behaviour of the trout,' he'd say of the Gravel Fly: 'Trout have to follow instead of waiting for the fly to float over them.'

The types of fly known as Variants he dressed and used in 1875 as wet flies; and after 1890 as dry flies. 'It is difficult to know who was the first to use or invent almost anything,' he said.

'Never disturb the water,' he told me, 'or imagine that all fish are on the other side. Keep out of sight. Have an eye for water. The large fish selects the best feeding place.'

He caught his biggest Brown Trout in a small river in Argyll, one mile above a brackish loch. The water was low and clear beneath a bright August sun. He saw a dimpling rise, cast over it with a Baigent's Brown – it rose, head and tail. In his words, 'It raced all over the pool, more by good luck than good management keeping clear of the bushes. It was too big for the net. I couldn't reach it with the short pocket gaff. A friend appeared who had caught many a salmon but had never gaffed one; he put the hook in at the first stroke but, anxious to clear the bushes, swung the fish too high and, slipping free, it fell into the water with a tremendous flop. Fortunately the cast held, and the second attempt brought to grass a short thick fish of six and three-quarter pounds in the pink of condition.'

Every fisherman must have known one special trout – perhaps the wily old fellow who lurks in the deep pool above the bridge under cover of bushes where it is impossible to reach him. Easy to think like a trout. A salmon? Unpredictable. Who knows what adventures *he* may have met on his journeys. We see him on his way back to the spawning beds to beget a new generation. What memories and instincts guide him there?

Again I look at the notes. 'They follow one another from pool to pool when ascending rivers, by instinct or out of sympathy who shall say? They congregate in places selected to their liking, follow each other round the pool and the jumping of one is followed by another: for what reason? I have often known the wrong salmon gaffed by mistake for the hooked fish, and the latter afterwards landed. Surely none of these instances had anything to do with the desire for food; call it sympathy, instinct, what you will.'

My father gaffed my first salmon for me, a twenty-two-pounder. A moment later I was into another; this time I called my mother – between us it got away.

This has been about the fisherman. In a drawer of a writing desk belonging to his mother, I found a list of the flowers of Holy Island, and a letter, dated September 27th, 1890, addressed to St. Mary's Vicarage, Berwick-on Tweed – 'My dear Mother, A little more good news for you. I have been fortunate enough to come out first among the M.D.'s and, in consequence, got the Gold Medal for being the

Dr. William Baigent with Anne

most distinguished graduate of the year. With much love, Your affectionate son. P.S. My essay on Multiple Peripheral Neuritis was spoken of highly by the examiners.'

He did the illustrations of the Fundus Oculi for Sir Thomas Oliver's book on lead poisoning.

He chose a country practice where there was a Cottage Hospital and he could practise surgery. Every patient was a friend.

He was Chairman of the Tees Fishery Board. He remembered as a boy the year when the Tees was frozen for weeks, and the joy of skating for miles on what seemed to him a new dimension.

He taught our eldest daughter to fish, and netted her first trout when she was four.

His book on Hackles is dedicated to 'The best companion an angler ever had – my wife'.

He died on April 12th, 1935.

Chapter Seven

FISHING IN PROSE AND VERSE

After the memoir I wrote about Father for *The Journal of The Fly-fishers' Club*, I became a regular contributor to this periodical during the 1970s and 1980s. More than twenty years later I am still writing for it. I have also contributed to *The American Fly Fisher*. What follows is a selection of my poetry and articles for these two journals.

TIME KEEPER

Telling the salmon, 'Seek your natal redd';
Guiding the gnat through metamorphic state;
Warning the adder, 'Time your skin to shed;
Snowdrop take spear! Pierce winter's armour plate.
Swallow fly north, there's no time for delay,
Your nest's still there, above the barnyard door,
Flycatchers are already on their way,
The curlew's left the coastline for the moor.'
Of all enigmas, what could be more strange,
We ask, what activitates Creation's clock?
What ratchet regulates the strokes that range
Through species that can swim, swarm, soar or flock?
Obeying, yet selective in their choice,
The dictates of a supramundane voice.

HEAR YOU THIS TRITON OF MINNOWS?
(Shakespeare, *Coriolanus*, III.i.88)

I came to the conclusion that a river accepted one or did not.

My father appeared to be on good terms with every river, and there were few North of the Humber that he had not fished.

Only the Don and the Tees went out of their way to persuade me that I was accepted in my own right, not just as my father's 'chela'. Twice when entirely alone on stretches previously unfamiliar, Moneymusk and Upper Brux, I was welcomed by part of a river to such an extent that fish ignored my presence. I experienced that same feeling of awe when swimming in Loch Fyne and finding myself in the middle of a school of porpoises; I could swear that they were amused by my alarm, and appeared desirous of playing a game with me, the porpoise equivalent of a Ring of Roses.

The Tees – always to my surprise and I think that of my father – yielded a fair harvest of salmon in unexpected places, rather than well-known pools and runs, where salmon had an unfair advantage because there was little room for manoeuvre owing to shelving rocks and overhanging trees and no chance to keep level.

In The Theatre in the Forest of Grizedale, listening to the renowned angler Arthur Oglesby, and watching his film-recording of the Spey, I realised what a dilettante I have always been: fortunately salmon were less sophisticated in the first half of the century – certainly angling was a less expensive pursuit. There can be few fathers today who casually send twenty-pound salmon to their children at school.

Most anglers will agree that every river has a genre peculiarly individual. Our little Beck is no exception. It is secret and hidden and only becomes visible at a bridge across a bridle road four miles from a village, where our beat ends and the Vicar's begins. One makes surreptitious casts over his pool to extend one's line.

On some rivers my father and I fished companionably in sight of one another, with my mother installed in a sheltered spot reading, or making dolls' clothes which imperceptibly progressed to become dresses for babies, so beautifully embroidered that I hope someday they may grace a museum.

Fishing the Beck one was entirely alone, no voice ever heard, not even a dog's bark, or the bleating of sheep; quite different from the Don which is the noisiest river I know, cries of oyster-catcher, redshank, rooks and lambs adding up to a choral symphony. The Beck itself drowned all other sounds, enclosed as it was by high banks and shrouded by willow and alder.

Only once did I experience a hatch of mayfly: quite different from a hatch of grannom on the Don. Do these immense hatches still occur? The first I encountered took me by surprise. Some illness had prevented me going back to school at the beginning of term: instead I went – for the first time – to Aberdeenshire with my parents. I was fishing the Rookery Stream below Keig Bridge when I became aware of a sense of expectancy, the river, a few minutes before apparently devoid of fish, beginning to stir. I turned, and wafting gently upstream came a grey mist. It carried on steadily, and then, deflected by the bridge, grannom settled on broom and gorse, on the stanchions of the bridge and on me.

The pool boiled with rises, great trout, appearing to my unaccustomed eyes akin to the rolling porpoises of Loch Fyne, though there was no mirth in their urgency as each leapt at the female grannom dapping her emerald eggs on the water. Standing in the midst of all this, casting wildly over rise after rise, one was oneself a participant in a tumultuous rhythm of life and death. Then it was over, only a few spent flies floating downstream, and the faintest dimple of a rise from already satiated trout.

A hatch of mayfly on the Beck was altogether different – more of a midsummer's dream, transforming the dark, sometimes rather menacing Beck into a fairyland of gossamer wings and leaping troutlets. It was at all times not merely a stream to be fished, it had a taste for the spectacular.

The day we went to have a final throw-in, knowing we could no longer visit it regularly, it pulled out all the stops in its register. The first fish that my husband hooked ran neither downstream nor up; it dived into the roots of a willow. I took the rod; there was nothing I could do but hang on while he clambered up the bank and undressed. It is no joke on a cold late September afternoon, plunging naked into a deep pool, groping blindly to retrieve a large trout, and if possible a fly, from a tangle of roots. He succeeded.

Unlike my father, he never carried a flask. A handkerchief is a poor substitute for a towel. We had a long drive ahead; we decided to call it a day. As he dressed, I dismantled the rod. We were both looking rather sadly towards the Corner Pool when it happened. It is something we have neither of us managed to explain to our satisfaction.

All trout are cannibal to some extent. Could this long lean black object that leapt from the pool be one? Dusk tends to exaggerate size: had I been asked to judge, I should have reckoned ten pounds. Take five away and there still remained a monster bigger than anything ever seen in the Beck. A Kraken, we agreed: Oliver Goldsmith maintained that to believe in one would be credulity, to reject the possibility of its existence would be presumption.

TO A LARVA RESCUED FROM A BUNCH OF CRESS

Larva! With a pinhead brain
Robing yourself in peacock train,
Garnered from root hairs of cress
To cloak your opaque nakedness:
Dowered with pebbles from a stream,
Masqued in patchwork colour scheme:
Arrived at your quiescent state
You dream away the winter night
Preparing for your nuptial flight.
While you pupate
I cogitate.
Your flair for your peculiar task
Prompts the innocent to ask –
Exile from a nameless rill,
Whence the well-spring of your skill?
Are constellations on their course
The fountain that fills full the source?

GOLDEN AGE OF ANGLING

This, to my mind, began with the emergence of the motor car at the beginning of the century. My father told me that before 1900 he cycled to his fishing at home and in Scotland. How he managed I cannot imagine; boots, waders, rod, basket, net; his pockets bulging with reel, cast box and a great red wallet containing flies which had once probably belonged to Great-Uncle George who, living on the banks of the Tees, had no problem of locomotion.

Father said it was a long dusty ride to the Beck, about eight or ten miles, after that several fields with fences and hedges to negotiate. He was adamant all his life about leaving no trace, causing no damage.

The car was heaven-sent; in it we stowed our tackle. Mother came with us to the Swale or Tees, and to every river in Scotland; but only occasionally to the Beck. Even without a bicycle it was a problem to get to the notice 'Private Fishing' nailed crookedly on a willow tree. There was a right of way through corn and hay fields, but we deemed it more tactful to cling to the bank – so overgrown we were not likely to disturb the trout. Scarlet pimpernel grew here, and some rare flower I cannot remember; it was a secret divulged to one botanist and she is long since dead.

Sheona's first salmon, a twenty-two pounder

Great-Uncle George flyfishing on the Tees

Arriving at the boundary I put up the two-piece greenheart rod, taking care that sand or soil did not get into the reel, threaded the line, learnt to tie on the cast. We clambered down the bank and I stood beside my father absolutely still. It was up-stream wet fly fishing in those early days. The flies, a March Brown, a Greenwell and probably an iron blue or olive dun.

Father knew the first pool would yield three trout, probably one quite large one, three quarters of a pound, or even a one-pounder. Where the stream flowed over a rock, he could be sure of two more. The next stretch was a dead loss, although it would have been possible to cast properly as there were fewer trees. Sand martins flew in and out of their nests in the bank, taking no notice of us. Usually we would see a flash of blue as the kingfisher streaked past.

It was at the corner pool that the excitement began. Father reckoned to get at least five trout here. They were strong and lively fish, there was no room for manoeuvre; besides, one didn't want to disturb the water. It was a case of reeling in quickly, taking out the hook gently (strange that one never wanted to hurt), a swift blow on the head, a glance to see the barb of each fly was intact, and another cast.

I began to fish when it was possible to get waders small enough to fit me: I'd be seven or eight I suppose, and was already tying my own flies, not because I wanted to, but because it was a way of life. It was what one did on Sunday afternoons in winter, sitting at my own table in the window beside Father. I was never as nimble as he was. He preferred dry fly to nymph, though he fished both. For him wings, woodcock or starling, stood upright, never went askew as mine did: he achieved a perfect figure of eight with his hackle, through the wings, round, back again. At this moment my waxed silk would break, and I'd have to start all over again. I hated cutting away the peacock quill body, the mallard tail, which I'd taken such trouble with; and the hackle I'd chosen with care. It never happened to Father, probably because he used even tension. A vice? Heaven forbid! The art of fly tying was to become ambidextrous, neat with one's fingers.

For the Beck I never had a rod equal to Father's greenheart: mine was good enough for a beginner but too long. It had been chosen for the Swale as well as the Beck.

I lost more flies among branches than I cared to divulge to Father, or even to remember now. When I'd really got the hang of it, I was left at the bridge to fish up alone, while Father went to the lower stretch.

There was one frightening pool. The water was deep – came over my waders; no birds sang there, the voice of the stream ceased to be companionable. Children don't talk of such things, but at last I told

Father, and was surprised when he said he felt exactly as I did at that pool. Primitive instinct probably, he explained: an enemy could get you easily there, the banks were so high, there was no way of escape.

The Beck trout were pink as sea trout, better eating than any from other streams or rivers. Dipped in 'best medium oatmeal' which Mother ordered from Edinburgh. Peppered, salted and fried on the enormous kitchen stove which had to be black-leaded every day. A kitchen glowing with brass warming pans and candlesticks. A dresser held willow pattern plates; there was an oak chest, a salt box, and a red tiled floor which, strange as it may seem, had to be washed with milk.

My mother made my first fishing jacket of waterproof material. It had four enormous pockets, and raglan sleeves in order that there should be no restriction to the arms when casting. It was far too large at the time, but it lasted for years – in fact, I still have it in the same drawer as my wedding dress. There was a little wrap-over mini-skirt to match. Considering we never saw a soul, and in any case the jacket was long, the latter appears to me today to have been unnecessary.

I can't remember how old I was when I acquired my Hardy rod and reel. I have this moment been inspecting them and trying, without success, to check the price of each in *Hardy's Angler's Guide 1925*. I do see, however, that 'Dr. Baigent's flies' were five shillings a dozen. In the bag beside the reel are some Alcock's brand-new 3-X casts, and dozens of small boxes with flies tied through the ages – strange to think that some of them are sixty or more years old.

I made one discovery for myself. The fly I really enjoyed tying was the red tag, because it required no wings. Father regarded this as a grayling fly, but I tried it on the Beck and trout leapt at it. What was its appeal, I wonder: the red flosstail, the peacock body, or was it in fact the hackle?

Father said, 'Think like a trout,' and I did. The trout part of me, by cunning and strength, managed to select the best feeding place where the current floated the choicest flies over my nose. I knew by instinct when there was likely to be a hatch of mayfly or march brown; as the females dipped on the water, laying their eggs, I became excited; if the fly's action was what I was used to, if it looked tempting, I'd seize it. The human part of me said, would I notice if its wings were starling or woodcock, its legs ginger or listed or blue? What was important was the buoyancy, the life-like behaviour of the fly.

As a human I chose hackles with care, noting the stiffness and the shape: there were capes in plenty, and though I experimented a little, I realized Father had an unerring eye for the most alluring, and never minded if a few hackles disappeared from his table.

I like to think the trout part of me will spend the last moments in life not in fear, but in fight for survival, without thought. If S.L. is at the other end of its line, the chances are ten to one in my favour and I shall live to fight another day.

As for the Golden Age, I imagine our thoughts, the trout's and my own, are almost identical: we remember the days when anglers were less thick on the ground, when rivers and streams were less polluted, when weed-killer had not been thought of, and flies were plentiful.

Perhaps for both of us, the Golden Age is when we were young.

GREENHEART

A short rod
Handy for the beck
Where a sideways flick
Of either wrist
Was for the most part
All that was required.

It had been his rod
Since he was a boy:
I was allowed to assemble it
Never permitted to fish with it:
As far as he was concerned
It was sacrosanct.

My rod was split-cane, whippy, too long for the beck.

What made his rod special?
Perhaps Great-Uncle George designed it
And that was why it retained its green heart.
Where water rippled over shallows,
In deep pools under willow and alder
It seemed to live.

When it became mine I lent it
And it was broken.

Kingfisher, dipper,
Scent of wild crushed mint remain.
Gone
The greenheart.

WAY TO THE SWALE

Where three roads met
He danced
Sad eyes
Clumsy
Shackled by his chains;
A bear
Led by Russians
In an English lane;
Verges blue
With cranesbill and butterflies.
The only other pilgrims
On the road that day
Were tinkers
Their lurchers cowering beneath flat carts,
Wary like their masters
Yet eyes, ears, nose keen
For sign of game
In rustling hedgerows and fields of ripening corn.
Pale giant bell-flowers
And viper's bugloss
Avenued the path
That led us to the gravel bed.
Does the uncherished chub
Still suck the olive dun
And grayling snatch at red tag?
(Peacock body, red hackled legs, tail of red floss silk.)
Today
Barley or rye may curtsey
Where once rogue ragwort blazed.
The corncrake
Wandering among withered water-weeds –
Unseen ventriloquist
His voice now close
Now far away
Has he too gone?
Paulinus if his spirit haunts the Swale
Does he note still water
Where the great pike lurks below the bridge?
Does he reckon barbel
Blessed as any trout?

The bear danced for us on our way to the Swale in 1906.

Concerning Paulinus, in 630 A.D. Gregory the Great wrote in an epistle to St. Eulogius, Patriarch of Alexandria: 'On the day of Christ's nativitie, he did regenerate by lively baptisme above ten thousand men, beside an innumerable multitude of women and children. Having hallowed and blessed the river, called in English Swale, the archbishop commanded by the voice of criers and maisters that the people should enter the river confidently, two by two, and in the name of the Trinitie baptise one another by turnes. Thus were they all borne againe with no lesse a miracle, than in times past, the people of Israel passed over the sea divided, and likewise Jordan when it turned backe; for even so, they were transported to the banke on the other side: and notwithstanding so deepe a current and channell, so great and so divers differences of sex and age, not one person took harme. A great miracle no doubt, but this miracle as it was, a greater pre-eminence doth surmount: in that all feebleness and infirmitie was laid off in that river; whosoever was sick and deformed returned out of it whole and reformed.'

THE DON

Waking in the morning, wondering if it is going to be a real fishing day – not too thundery, not too bright, hoping for a spot of rain with sun bursting through the clouds – warmth after rain prompting a hatch of fly.

Breakfast – porridge and a bowl of cream eaten standing, Scottish fashion, a dish of trout, bacon and eggs, honey in the comb, oatcake, and every variety of what old Miss Spence of the Forbes Arms calls 'soft pieces'.

Having donned boots and waders we look at our casts – two at least should be new; 3-X if the river is low. Flies – a selection of Baigent's Browns and Variants, perhaps one or two black spiders, and olive and blue duns.

The line has been left to dry the night before. One has to remember to hold it taut between the little and ring finger as one winds it. It won't do to find it in a ravel as one hooks a four-pounder. Floating oil, net scissors, and the sandwiches and we are ready; my father in the car in a frenzy of impatience saying the rise will be over and the day wasted.

Leaving the car at Keig Bridge, we scramble down the bank and walk up-stream, keeping out of sight, yet my father never missing a rise, an oyster-catcher's nest, or a reed warbler's, in the rushes; and a baby plover or two. If – when we get to Broom Brae – trout are rising, we put up our rods and unwind our casts in a state of wild excitement.

My father steps into the water without causing a ripple. He rarely wades far in (saying of inexperienced anglers that they stand where their flies should be), the first cast, a short one, to see that flies are floating well and to wash away surplus oil (two flies, a Baigent's Brown on the point, the dropper a Variant), the next cast over the exact spot, letting the fly drop lightly on the water an inch above the nose of a rising trout, or where he knows one will lie. The big trout chooses the best place where a submerged boulder makes an eddy and the current carries flies over its head.

I see it happening – see the fly sucked under the surface – 'Got him!'; a whirr of the reel and the trout is at the far side of the river; my father climbs up the bank; from the first minute he has the trout under control, he keeps level with it, lowering the point of the rod when it leaps out of the water. It's beginning to tire. My father un-hooks his net from the button hole in the lapel of his Burberry, brings his fish to the top of the water in a calm place near the bank, slides the net under the surface, lets the fish float downstream over it, a quick controlled movement, and the trout is at his feet. He knocks it on the head with a sharp stone before removing the fly, and pops it into his mackintosh-lined pocket. He wipes his fly, dips it into the bottle of floating oil, and he's ready for the next cast.

He covers little water, often fishing not more than three pools a day. His record – twenty-nine trout, twenty-seven pounds. His gift is in making trout rise to his fly when water is low and fish not in a tak-ing mood.

Grannom hatch about the middle of May, usually during the first warm spell after rain. They come floating in a cloud. For days they can be seen clinging to bushes of broom. The females have a soft vel-vety emerald tail. This is the oviduct from which they drop their eggs on the water. When the grannom is 'on', the river is alive with rising fish; big ones come up at one's feet. One casts madly, the water is so black with fly that the chance of a fish taking an artificial one seems remote, yet it will go hard if one does not get a basket.

Today we have a strange encounter with a big trout. I have bor-rowed my father's new Hardy rod and cast over a rising fish, 'a small one' I think as I reel him in. To my amazement he sails serenely to the far side of the river. An enormous fellow is holding my little chap by the middle, crosswise. My father wades into the river with his net. I reel in gently. With a swoop my father flings net and trout on to the bank. His description of it 'not very large!', but a fine plump fish with a small head, in grand condition, weighing over four and a quarter pounds, with none of the supposed cannibalistic appearance about him. 'All trout are cannibals,' he adds, 'the one so called is probably out of condition, aged and like an old lion has difficulty in making a living, or the food supply may be short. He is neither more nor less a cannibal than his brethren.'

The Sabbath – a long walk to the kirk with Mr. Strachan. The precentor holds his tuning fork to his ear to get the pitch for the first psalm. It's a poor sermon that doesn't last an hour – Mr. Strachan places his watch beside his Bible in order to time it, we pull down the blinds of the window of our pew to keep the sun out of our eyes. 'O Thou,' says the Minister, 'Who paintest the polyanthus purple.' Pure poetry never to be forgotten.

Spinners in a spiral dance over the bridge. Scent of wallflowers. The Don in May and June.

RIVER MUSIC

Voices re-echo through the seven seas:
Beinn Bhuidhe's, and the grannom-haunted Don
Drown ocean moanings with their clarion
Of gravel redd and myrtle-scented breeze:
Insistent themes that summon, lure and tease
The urgent salmon as he journeys on
Towards the beckoning halcyon,
Beyond the opulence of ocean's ease:
Where music changes to a carillon
And river diapason tones exalt.
Fall's thunderous reed-stops make the pulses sing:
The course almost completed, seal threats gone,
He forges strength to stage the last assault
To reach the source whence Delphic voices spring.

COUNTING THE SPOTS

Willows and alder formed an impenetrable barrier; the banks were steep; even when the river was low, the water too deep for wading. In the pool above the bridge, four sea trout were poised motionless among roots and submerged branches. The sun was so bright that their shadows on the silted bed were more easily discernible than the trout themselves. My father, although he knew it was impossible to cast a fly, stealthily approached the first bush; the fish appeared to take no notice; he moved another inch, and imperceptibly they faded away.

We went downstream: fishing up, we were back at the bridge in an hour; the trout were in the same place, motionless as before. 'We'll outwit them yet,' murmured my father. At dusk he cut and trimmed one bush – just a little; the trout would still have a sporting chance.

Next day, from a safe distance, I watched him approach the pool, crouching so low 'his heart resented being pressed heavily to the ground in the moments of anticipation' preparatory to making a cast. There was not a trout to be seen. They had been there for days; the slight trimming of the bush had affected the ambient air, and that season they never returned.

Further up the river was a pool noted for large sea trout; difficult to approach, bushes on one side, an overhanging ash tree on the other; the bank almost perpendicular, about eight feet high. I remember that bank well: one day when the river was in spate it collapsed and cascaded me into the pool. My waders filled with water and made it nearly impossible to swim. How could the sun shine and the birds sing, I remember wondering, when I am about to drown? The current swept me into still water and within reach of a branch; dripping and frightened I clambered out and went to find my father. But this is a digression: it is the story of my father and of one particular sea trout that I want to tell.

'I approached most carefully,' he said. 'He was lying nearer than I had anticipated and in shallower water; alarmed, he moved away. Would he come back? The sun was bright, no breeze, not a ripple: a parched leaf now and then fell with a crackling dryness on the water and remained there motionless; no current at this side of the pool. Mid-day, and a rest, standing in the pool in the shade, eating sandwiches to while away the time. The rod was ready, a lucky snatch cast would cover the fish if he came back.

'Presently he returns to the centre of the river, but is out of reach: slowly he comes nearer, every spot is visible, the respiratory movement of his gill covers are plainly seen; he is at least eight or nine pounds. He is now in the same position as when disturbed, about two rods' length away, as still as a log. A difficult cast on account of overhanging branches, but the trout can't see one against the dark background with blazing sunlight on the water. With the gentlest movement the fly is flicked, but the fish glides away before it touches the water; he has seen the gut.

'Next day the sun still shines out of a cloudless sky. A small wingless black fly with a tinge of red in the hackle, sparsely dressed, is in readiness, a trout cast made: it will float well and remain on the surface in the still water an endless time. There is no sign of the fish. Presently he appears on the deeper side, settles in the middle; slowly he comes nearer, almost under the hackled floater. He takes no notice; minutes pass, does he see the fly? The rod point is given the gentlest trembling movement, the fly responds with a lifelike quiver. It attracts his attention, he appears to move his eyes without his body. He raises himself like a submarine coming to the surface, and without alarm lazily noses the fly; there is an infinitesimal opening of the mouth and the fly disappears: in an instant he reaches the deeper side and shelter of the friendly bushes; then with one wild shaking jump, he snaps the cast and is seen no more. Any regret is compensated by experience gained.'

The following year my father captured one of the sea trout from Maam Bridge – an episode he was never allowed to forget. 'Where,' he asked, as we met for dinner, 'is your mother?' We looked at him in consternation: we had suggested that she should come home with us but, 'No,' she had replied, 'Your papa will be tired, there are all those gates to open; I will wait for him.' Between us we had left her behind.

As we rushed for the car to go to her rescue, we met her, white with exhaustion and anger. She had walked eight miles with many a detour to avoid Highland cattle. We were in the clear: it was my father who was in trouble; so engrossed had he been, fighting once more – in his mind – the battle with a sea trout who for three years had challenged his skill and ingenuity, he had failed to notice my mother as she gathered up the paraphernalia of part-time ghillie, and set off home without her, his head obviously in the clouds. So shocked was he by his absentmindedness and momentary lack of thought for his wife, that ever afterwards he gave those sea trout a wide berth – in fact the victory was theirs, not his.

My father never guessed that the glen, once the haunt of Rob Roy and eagle, would one day be the site of a Hydro Electric station: that the track, skirting the Dubh Loch, fringed with water flag and bulrush, becoming ever rockier and narrower until it petered out among bog myrtle, cotton grass and heather, would become a tarmacadamed highway: that the mewing of buzzards would be drowned by the rumbling of lorries. Could my father have foreseen this, I think he would have rejoiced, as I find unexpectedly I do, that the sea trout whose spots he was able to count lived a little longer to enjoy and remain a part of the magic world of Glen Shira.

SALMON

Do you hear
The crunch of icebergs,
Conversation of whales,
The siren song of your
Own river summoning you,
The voice that will guide you
Past mouths of alien waterways
Until you recognise music
You knew as smolt?
Do you remember
Each pool, each run?
When you lie a shadow
Beneath the Force of Carlunnan
Do you look through froth
Effervescing above you
To rocks smoothed by centuries
Seemingly impregnable?
Does the voice direct you
To the first cranny
From whence you may slither and swim
Through rainbow spray
To the plumed crest
And gravel redd beyond?

The river snakes its way
Through peat bog
Fragrant with myrtle
Starred with asphodel and cotton grass –
Kingdom of Cruach Mhor.

FONS ET ORIGO

Never forget the primal source
    Half hidden under moss and peat
In an attempt to plot a course.

Meandering through thyme and gorse
    The infant river at our feet,
Never forget the primal source.

Renounce regret and vain remorse
    When floods prevail, or hail and sleet
In the attempt to plot a course.

When Lime-Kiln Pool meets Black-Sills Force
    And spray is rainbowed in the heat
Never forget the primal source.

It may require increased resource
    When torrent turns to glassy sheet
In the attempt to plot a course.

When peat meets salt, fearing perforce
    The clangour of the bell-buoy's beat,
Never forget the primal source
In the attempt to plot a course.

SAINT ANTHONY PREACHED TO THE FISHES
AND WAS HEARD WITH ATTENTION

Montpellier he'd been to and Toulouse
And now was on his way to Padua.
To rest his aching feet, beside a stream
Under a shady tree he chose to while an hour away.
Idly watching the rings of rising fish,
'Come listen to my sermon, Trout,' he said,
'Here in this peaceful vale where you're my flock,
I'll speak of virtues you and I both share:
Faith, your hope that there may be a hatch of fly:
Fortitude, when fortune does not come our way.'
Breaking his bread he threw pieces
To the waiting fish below, as he'd been wont
To do in Lisbon long ago. He laughed, 'I hope
The folk of Padua will be attentive,
Ready to accept my gifts as you.
Maybe I'll preach of this idyllic spot,
Where you, my finny friends, pursue your course,
Accepting with simplicity your lot,
Receiving strength from your Ligurian source:
So may we all resist false lures, nor fear
Impending drought, to live in innocence and peace
As you do, Trout.'

Chapter Eight

LIVING AND THINKING

When I was not writing about fishing, events of everyday life intervened. While washing up, I asked myself, why write? No-one can stop thinking. Ideas bottled up eventually burst forth. Speech may irritate or bore. There is no compulsion to read.

THOUGHTS

Thoughts unattended
Die, like flowers neglected
In an empty vase.

They come unannounced:
Fugitive, ephemeral,
Thoughts from the unknown.

Capture them, hold on!
Elusive as dreams, these thoughts;
Wayward as children.

Like mayfly they mate;
Their offspring become caddis.
Will they hatch next Spring?

And where shall I be?
The universal question,
Unanswered, unknown.

Old people sitting round a room – they've reached the state they had hoped would never arise: they have become a burden. How did their parents and grandparents cope? There were cousins, nieces, widowed sisters, willing to barter liberty for a secure home. Now there is Art Class on Monday, Keep Fit Tuesday, a lecture on Thursday. Friday? 'We may be able to come for a few minutes on Friday.' They in their turn will grow old. I've just come across this poem, written when the grandchildren were small, and it strikes me it's just like us.

IMMORTELLES

Honesty with her whispering papery pods,
You with your Japanese lanterns
Dangling from stiff stems.
I do not like you.
I borrowed your Aladdin lamps
For the Christmas tree:
Against its dark foliage
You shone.
You had your innings – twelve days.
For five months, I've watched you
Gathering dust.

Spring is here with the forsythia
And daffodils:
You – how can I dump you
On the compost,
Remembering?

Next October
Will you be standing bravely upright
In a jam jar
Tucked between tins of dog food,
Proclaiming
'We are the Immortelles.'
You glowing, while Honesty
Nods her silly silvery head?

A house full of dead flowers – I feel better when I summon the energy to throw the withered ones away. Then I return to old diaries and the computer.

It is odd the way the mind turns from past to present. The pieces one picks up are like bits of a jigsaw and it's fun finding a place for them and seeing a picture emerge.

A tower, a lighthouse – they must be universal images. I dream of the latter with an outside circular stair. Waves rage round rocks at its base. I climb, clinging to a rail, fragile as a spider's thread.

When the jigsaw's finished, will that be the centre piece? Or will there be a more comfortable homely one? Portrait of a family?

Meanwhile, here's a bit of chimney, here a bit of tree and lots of garden: let's concentrate on Wraysholme.

FRIDAY THOUGHTS
(helping Oliver to sweep the chimney)

House of my dreams, walls of jasper,
Windows double-glazed, no corners.
No wires to trip over, no pipes to freeze,
Warmed by perpetual sun.

Meanwhile the gas man cometh not:
My loved one produces a sweep's brush
With dozens of joints.
He disconnects the pipe,
Removes the ancient gas stove
(Among the debris, a dead mouse)
And begins to clean the chimney.

An aide required. I go outside.
A moment of acute anxiety –
Will the brush emerge
From the chimney known as the Eiger?
It does!

Indoors flue rods stretch
Snake-wise from room to room.
'Shall I help?' I ask.

Does any woman understand
The mechanism of a screw?
Left? Right? Try both.
Disaster!

The brush remains aloft,
A trunkless head.

My loved one is aghast.
Shall I call the police?
The fire brigade?
The undertaker!

Around midnight he arrives
With a posse of contractors.
No moon, no star; not even a flashlight.
Our courageous undertaker ascends the Eiger.

We, the assistants and I, stand in pitch darkness. Waiting.
Footsteps descend the ladder – dare we hope? All is well!
A hurdle in the course of a marriage negotiated.
Thank you, St. Anthony! Thank you, Mr. Edmondson!

GARDENS

1 *Redwood Tree*

House completed – perfect with pitch-pine panelling.
They planted a seedling
Outside a Southern window.
The tree grew;
Beneath its branches
Children played,
Cortèges waited.
A tree-creeper
Explored its soft resilient bark.
It comes closer;
Its roots
Find their way
Beneath foundations.
The house
Trembles.

***

Convolvulus triumphantly
Blowing its own trumpet
Through spikes of berberis.
Goosegrass strangling
Alstromeria and phlox.
Buddleia shimmering with
Peacocks and Tortoiseshells
While Goldfinches feast
On poppy seeds.
The Redwood stands guardian
Merging its branches
With Orion and the Pleiades.

99

2 *Hortus Conclusus*

Philadelphus
Against a lichened wall
Where jewelled gleams
Of finches fly
Feasting on seeds of mid-July.

Drift of falling petals
Counting the hours
Of summer gone.

Scent of syringa
Weaving
Separate gardens*
Into one.

*Northallerton and Wraysholme

3 *Garden in Late Summer*

Keith has cut the grass,
Has raked the gravel,
The garden is at peace,
Except for jackdaws.
Eleven o'clock at night
They mutter in the rookery:
This time-sharing arrangement
Is of long standing. Rooks
Rear their young, depart,
Jackdaws take over,
Spilling onto our roof
Where they squabble and squawk
And fall down chimneys.
'Did you fall, or were you pushed?'
We ask, when they are safely ensconced
In a duster: their eyes look daggers,
So do their beaks. They fly off
On strong wings, and hold angry
Meetings in the sycamore
As if it were our fault and they

Were prepared to take revenge.
We had a tame jackdaw long ago,
He was a friendly bird.
One bird, one human can come
To terms: gangs threaten.

4 *Millans Park Safari*

Once it was the doctor's house,
The door opened by Eleanor
In cap and apron.
Sweet peas grew in the garden:
Spotted flycatchers
Launched their young
From the montana
Beneath the nursery window.

The new owners are animal lovers:
Seventeen cats, numerous rabbits,
Two dogs and a tortoise roam in
Their garden, and those of their
Neighbours. Householders who
Cherish rare gentians complain;
Some write Solicitor's letters,
Others summon the Pest Controller.
One is not displeased: she is
Partial, she says, to rabbit pie.

Willy nilly we have become part of the safari.
A proud bantam escorts his wives and chickens,
Sometimes with ducklings in tow, down the drive;
A silver pheasant adds exoticism to the precincts.

Swifts, swallows, martins, unaware of change
Follow their unfailing pattern, swooping low
Over the lawn on cloudy days, soaring
Almost out of sight when the sun shines.
Paradise is never wholly lost.

5 *Gardening Together*

Nettles and ground elder
Flourish
Beneath sycamores
Heavy with late summer;
Browning buddleias
Still attract
Peacocks and Tortoiseshells,
Informed by instinct
That nectar gathered today
Improves the chances
Of survival.

6 *Villanelle*

The blackbird in the holly tree
  An armour-plated site has won,
He greets the spring and so do we.

I sip my morning cup of tea
  And watch – my morning's chores undone –
The blackbird in the holly tree.

A heron flaps across the scree;
  His fishing day has just begun,
He greets the spring and so do we.

Bother beds, breakfast, drudgery;
  Oh! heavenly day, we've got the sun,
The blackbird in the holly tree.

A morning when all things we see,
  Creatures that fly, that crawl, that run,
Enjoy the spring and so do we.

In dawn's soft haze it seems to me
  That May a magic web has spun –
The blackbird in the holly tree
Enjoys the spring, and so do we.

7 *I Love My Love with an S*

I love my garden with an S because I enjoy seclusion.
I hate it because stooping – to sow seeds – makes me stiff.
Strawberries surrender their sweetness to slugs.
Sycamore seeds scatter themselves indiscriminately
Overshadowing salvia and spiraea.
Scent of syringa,
Sum and substance of
Summer.

THE HOUSE

We are its mirror image
The aga grows cold:
We take its temperature
And ours!
A feeble flame flickers:
We take heart.

We love our house.
Its pitch pine panelling,
Its proportions,
Its balcony.

Age and the elements
War against it:
Frost, thaw,
Drip, drip, drip:
Our tears flow.

Poor house, poor us.
'Thoo's had thi day'
They say hereabouts –
Though they can't
Be sure.

The Aga has been converted to gas! (1985)
Now we have a new one! (1989)

U.F.O.

When he retired in 1959 Oliver became an amateur organist. He liked to arrive at the Church early in order to put up the hymns and practise the voluntary.

One Sunday at Brathay, we found a group of parishioners gathered on the steps of Holy Trinity gazing skywards at an object unlike anything ever seen before. How to describe it? It seemed to be a huge triangular stationary aeroplane gleaming as an aeroplane gleams in the setting sun.

We stood on the steps until 9.29. The service began at 9.30. At 10.40 the service over, it was still there. On the way home we passed little groups of people looking up to the sky.

The Langdales are not visible from Millans Park, they are obscured by Loughrigg, but after the car was in the garage we could still see the Object. This may give some indication of its height.

'What do you think it is?' I asked a young man who was gazing at the sky.

'I'm in the R.A.F.,' he said, with a Scottish accent. 'I've never seen the like before; it could be something from the Met. Office,' he added doubtfully.

Reluctantly I went into the house for lunch. At 2 p.m. the sky in the North West was obliterated by mist, caused by the Object, one wondered? Elsewhere it was clear.

At that time there was a doctor, a keen naturalist, who knew the day, the hour, the first swallow, willow wren and cuckoo arrived; when to listen for curlew flying inland to their nesting ground. He missed nothing. I spoke to him about the Object; he was unexpectedly, inexplicably, angry. 'Don't be so foolish,' he said.

Although there was a paragraph in the *Manchester Guardian* the next morning to the effect that the Met. Office disclaimed all knowledge I refrained from speaking about it; we were comparative newcomers, and I feared another rebuff.

Years later an ex-Wing Commander said he had seen it from Storrs, had rung up the R.A.F. and the War Office, but it was Sunday!

As I write I ask myself, 'did the Vicar not see it?' (He died some years ago.) Our present one would have mentioned it in his sermon, if not before! Did we not believe our own eyes? Did no-one else ask the doctor if he'd seen it? Was everyone afraid of being thought credulous and foolish? The Wing Commander and the *Manchester Guardian* are the only proof I have that I actually did see An Unidentified Object. I must add it looked uncommonly like a Flying Saucer.

February 5th 1993: Today I remembered the story of the U.F.O. 'Why not ask Wing Commander Thomas?' I asked myself. So I did. This is his story.

One Sunday morning in the sixties he was sitting in the garden and happening to look up saw a luminous object in the sky. 'A parachute. A balloon?' he wondered. 'Objects in the sky do not remain motionless. I was puzzled,' he continued. 'I rang up the R.A.F. Authorities at Preston (part of the Radar chain for Commercial Flying) and the Police Station.' They had already been alerted.

'How high was it?' I asked.

'Altitude? 15,000 to 20,000 feet,' he replied.

He lives at Storrs near Windermere. I first saw it at Brathay. To me it seemed the size of a two-seater aeroplane; solid, triangular and – as he said – luminous.

'Did you see it depart?' I asked.

'A cloud obscured it from view,' he replied. 'It was reported in some newspaper the following morning,' he told me.

It was probably not the 'Manchester Guardian'.

To have it within our grasp for several hours and not even a photograph!

VISITS AND VISITORS

The Bridge Club met on Wednesdays. Oliver had never even played 'snap' before retiring; now he acquired an enormous American bridge manual, from which he worked out his own conventions. This made him a challenging partner as no-one ever understood the intention of his calls. Yet he was rather pleased when he won the Silver Slam Cup two years running!

It was difficult for me to concentrate on bridge when I wanted to write – it didn't matter if it was prose or poetry. What's more, people tended to turn up out of the blue. Here's a piece about those days.

Oliver brings home organ players, who drift into church while he is practising. They all seem to have large families and come from the U.S.A., Scandinavia, sometimes Africa. Fiona produces folk who she thinks require mothering. The latest was an Australian girl she met on Loughrigg.

Sometimes I feel I might as well be working behind the refreshment bar in Victoria Station, but a glance through any window dispels 'sorry for oneself' thoughts. It's not just the garden, but Loughrigg, Fairfield, Wansfell, the Rothay and Stock Ghyll never looking the same for more than one minute. Clever Fiona to have found such a spot.

Today, a heron flaps over the park towards Brathay. One dark, cloudy night in late February, Eric Fothergill came to us – had we heard curlew, sandpiper and redshank flying inland to their nesting grounds? Pipings and whisperings in the dark and the feeling of unseen masses overhead. I've heard it once before, in about 1905, when Father woke me and held me in his arms to listen.

We woo spotted woodpeckers by hanging mutton fat on the balcony. Nuthatches and treecreepers are partial to the Redwood and there is one slow-worm and a family of hedgehogs in the garden.

Very early one morning there was a red deer eating roses. The badger may visit us often, but we've only seen him once: Anne tumbled over him in the dark when he was being chased by her dog.

On a winter night, Spruce woke me, barking violently and leading me to the front door. I turned on the light to see hundreds of eyes shining like little lamps. Snow was about a foot deep, so I suppose that had enabled a flock of sheep to leap the wall. They must have been hungry, but I couldn't think of anything suitable for them. Next morning when I told Oliver, he said, 'You should have driven them away.' In a nightie, in a snow storm, in the middle of the night? He might have done so. In the morning, they had gone.

We feel we are living in the depths of the country, yet five minutes walk away, there are shops, a pillar box and a village full of long-haired hikers. We hear church bells when the wind is in the right direction. There are far too many jackdaws and they drown the songs of other birds.

INVASION FAIRIELD

Neolithic man first roamed her slopes	*2000 B.C.*
His blood maybe it was that stained	
The sundew red.	
With glacial stones from Brathay's bed	
The Romans built Galava in her shade.	*A.D. 80*

Came Anglian with his horse-drawn plough	*A.D. 540 – 700*

Tilling land made fertile by her becks.
Next raiding Viking
Bringing crafts and skills,
Working iron for their swords,
Adding Scandinavian words –
Skali, gafl, knutr, hyjartar, gringler, ghyll.

Then the conquest of the Norman
With the Monastery and Pele:
Hamlets growing, commerce flowing
Through his industry and zeal.
Yet the Border still unsettled
As attacking Scots converge
To waste Furness, ravage homesteads,
Over Solway Bay they surge.

Now invasion comes by highway –	*1974*

More insidious malaise –
Where pack horses once would stumble
Juggernauts to Windscale rumble
Changing gear on Dunmail Raise.

Heron Pike, Great Rigg, and Hart Crag
Quarter your heraldic shield;
Through the troubled tide of ages
Your escutcheons blaze FAIR FIELD.

Now the juggernauts use the M6 and nuclear waste is transported by rail.

Sheepdog trials are held at the foot of Fairfield. There we meet 'The
County' at a luncheon party, sometimes in Mrs. Curwen's house,
sometimes in her marquee. The latter is no ordeal. One sees lots of

people whom one knows, there is an abundance of food and drink, one can actually sit back and watch the trials in comfort or slip away and mingle with the crowd.

Luncheon in Mrs. Curwen's house, which is comparatively small, is necessarily select: everyone is related distantly to everyone else – except ourselves. We wonder why on earth we are invited. I am reminded of the balls of one's youth when the chaperones sat, magnificent in pearls and tiaras, aloof, keen eyes noting what went on, who was dancing with whom. We were small fry and passed unnoticed.

Here in Mrs. Curwen's house, we stand in the doorway of the dining room – I am rather shaken, having fallen down a step and sent a grandfather clock rocking – everyone is talking animatedly in little groups, except for the eagle-eyed elderly sitting with their backs to the wall.

We don't know a soul. Is Oliver saying to himself, as I am, 'Have we not met ambassadors; disported ourselves in foreign countries representing Great Britain?' There we had a label, here we have not. How to break through the divide that separates them from us? Hallie's advice comes to our aid. Find some poor lonely sap, talk to him with animation, look as if you are enjoying yourself and others will gather round.

At this party, if you are not an Etonian, did not come over with William the Conqueror and have not the fortune to be in the Brigade of Guards, you might as well be dead. In time, we discover ordinary human beings whose children are impossible, marry the wrong people, become artists or something equally disreputable.

Colour will go from life when we become equal. What is it about Mrs. Curwen that makes her interesting? We go for drinks. She is wearing heavy boots to protect her ankles from the teeth of her Scottie. The scene is like one from *Ruddigore*. Ancestors look down from heavy gold frames onto Chippendale and Hepplewhite furniture, protected by wire netting because Brockie is a gnawer of table and chair legs, as well as ankles. We drink whisky in a sort of elegantly furnished hencoop.

'Lely,' says Mrs. Curwen as we admire one of the portraits, 'made all his women look bitchy.'

Phoebe rang to say would I go to Grasmere Church to hear Jonathan Wordsworth, and she'd call at 7.30 p.m. How can anyone find anything fresh to say about W.W.? Jonathan excellent. Made one see him as an extraordinarily powerful and religious poet, choosing odd prosaic symbols. W.W. waiting for the coach to take him home from school, sitting under a wall. Nothing but wall, a thorn tree, a solitary sheep. Ten days later, all he'd been looking forward to ceased to be, his father dead. With what skill Jonathan ties this up with 'Tintern', the Lucy poems and *The Prelude*.

Church full of Wordsworths, living and dead. Richard (glamorous) part of the festival. Mary Henderson and her husband there. Phoebe has been going through the family tree – all those bishops. Such a physically, as well as mentally, vigorous lot, and all entirely different in their approach both to their ancestor and life in general. Richard spends much time in the States; Mary is at Rydal Mount at the moment. She and some of the family came to us on Boxing Day. A son-in-law complained that he'd been made to change into tidy clothes only to find his host descending from the roof, looking disreputable in a peculiarly unbecoming red pullover – a Christmas present.

PEACE AND GOODWILL

'It is rather a delicate matter,' said the voice. The heart of anyone must sink when hearing these words, especially the heart of someone who has any connection, however remote, with the Church.

I am the wife of an amateur organist. Every man, when he retires, should have a hobby if he wishes to retain the affection of his spouse. Playing the organ would appear to be a fairly harmless pursuit. It gets the beloved out of the house into the safe precincts of the church. Visiting organists of different nationalities (the female of that species do not present a serious danger) can be regaled with a glass of sherry and a card at Christmas. The hours of practice – what a godsend they are: the beloved 'there', occupied, content, above all tackling something new. The challenge of music, church music in particular, encompasses ideals, ambition (to improve), compassion and faith.

The other characters in my story are the Vicar, the Churchwarden, and members of the congregation of a small church on the outskirts of the parish. The problem which has arisen seems on the surface to be a simple one. Should there, or should there not, be hymns at the Communion Service on Christmas Day?

The Churchwarden says there have always been hymns on Christmas Day. Without hymns, it would not seem to be Christmas. The

Vicar, who will be fifty next month, has, I suspect, been told by his doctor to take things more quietly. Midnight Mass, three services in quick succession; it is not surprising that he should wish to cut one of them short in order to have a breathing space. What is more, I think he had in mind the welfare of his ninety-year-old organist when he suggested 'a plain service'.

To return to the telephone message and 'that delicate matter'. In replying, I murmured something about 'Peace and Goodwill'. 'There'll be no Peace and Goodwill as far as I'm concerned if we don't have hymns,' said the Churchwarden. There the matter rested. We had hymns.

THE TREE

Denuded of its baubles last Twelfth Night
And planted once again, how it did flout
The winter snow, the bitter frost's sharp bite,
Wild gales of spring, and the late summer's drought?
Today, December Seventeenth, it stands
Upright, its branches sparse – some dead – but these
We trim away, and now a few fresh strands
Of green appear. Not one of those fine trees
Selected to adorn a stately hall:
A humble gift looking so frail and small
This living tree that bears the Christ child's name.

Phyl gave us the tree in 1975. We planted it in the garden and I wrote this in 1976. We have left it in peace for two years and given it lots of peat and it still flourishes.

1989 – it has grown enormous!

JOSEFINA DE VASCONCELLOS

Age, that is to say Old Age, is becoming the 'in thing'. It is edging its way into the news; there is to be a university course on ageing. Everyone has witnessed age in various forms; those who have experienced it are unlikely to have an honours degree in the subject.

Talking of age, where does one begin? I won't think of people who have had strokes, are blind, deaf, have arthritis or cancer. I'll write of Josefina (de Vasconcellos) who is nearly ninety and an internationally known sculptress. She has just finished *The Holy Family* for Manchester Cathedral. Joseph having delivered the Babe is holding Him in his arms. Mary is leaning against Joseph's shoulder, exhausted yet full of wonder. A sleeping lamb lies at her feet.

This is a moment of serenity and family love, before the arrival of shepherds and kings. Yet Josefina is not satisfied. 'The Babe looks cross,' she says. 'Joseph has washed Him in cold water; and he's a bit incompetent about swaddling clothes.' She goes down on her knees. Does the Babe smile at her? When she rises the little face is contented, at peace. Revelations come to Josefina.

Her studio is perched on the edge of a rock above Stock Ghyll. Once a few unwary steps could have sent one hurtling over a precipice; now a wrought-iron railing provides safety and access to an arched terrace that is a near miracle, and a paradise for birds. Under a canopy of wisteria and montana families of wagtails, blackbirds, robins and tits ponder a minute before venturing into the studio. Soon they pluck up courage and in no time take possession, demanding Wensleydale cheese.

How can any one person be endowed with so many talents? Art, music, poetry, dance and a remarkable ability to plan and command! I haven't mentioned half her gifts. She can create out of thin air a hat, a dress; flowers grow for her. Coincidences occur in her concerns that would be unbelievable in fiction.

We met Josefina and Delmar Banner in their old farmhouse home on the side of Lingmoor, when she was designing apparatus to enable disabled children to experience dramatic movement and we have been friends ever since.

Chapter Nine

BRANCHES OF ONE TREE

Angus, Jane and Sue, seven, five and three. Never had I known more enchanting children, but what could I give them for breakfast? 'I can't eat eggs,' said Angus. Jane: 'I don't like porridge.' Sue merely shook her head. 'If you could choose anything in the world to eat, what would it be?' I asked. The answer came in unison, 'We can't tell you, it would be far too expensive.' 'Try,' I suggested. 'Bacon and fried pineapple.'

Feeling like a fairy Godmother and with heartfelt relief, I turned to the Aga and in a few minutes had the joy of seeing three well-behaved children attacking a hearty breakfast. They can't always have been good. I remember saying to Sue, 'What would you do if I was a cross grandmother?' 'We wouldn't come and see you,' she replied, amazed by such a foolish question.

Mother was the greatest influence in the first quarter of my life – she was always right, really and truly. So there was no need to question anything. Father taught me but he did not influence me. Oliver an influence? It never occurred to me. Only after his death did Anne become my life saver.

The grandchildren have sent me into reverse. They make me question, they make me laugh. I see life and history in a new light. It is a comfortable feeling this – that we are branches of one tree.

Angus, Jane and Susan Clare,
What were our dreams and hopes for you
When you were six and four and two?
In fact, there wasn't time to spare
(Cooking, washing, brushing hair)
To wonder what would be your fate
When you were four and six and eight.

At eight and six and four you were
Not very different from before:
Just as clever, just as fair –
What are grandpas, grannies for
If not to spoil and to adore?

Eight years later …

A rainbow-knitted woollen square
Lies crumpled on a kitchen chair.
'That,' said F., 'a counterpane
For Angus, Susan Clare or Jane.'

'It's far too small for any bed!'
'Oh, no! It's for a cot,' she said.
'A cot?' 'Yes, for a baby, see!
I wonder which of all the three
Will have one first and will it be
A boy or girl?'
'Heavens! Your mind does leap ahead!'
'I like to be in time,' she said.

'Why, Angus is not seventeen,
Susan twelve and Jane fourteen.'
'It's nice to think of babies here –
Babes like Angus, Jane and Clare.'

Like F. sometimes we too dream dreams
Of Wraysholme bursting at the seams,
Again shrill voices before dawn;
Races, and high jumps, on the lawn.

No, things are better as they are
Just Angus, Jane and Susan Clare:
Nice when children come by train,
Angus, Jane, Susan, Jane's friend Jane.
Let people not grow up too soon,
Clocks be content to stop at noon.

We'd like to keep it always March
When tasselled buds adorn the larch;
The spruce is just a misty blue
And Spring's a promise not yet due.

Too soon this month will pass away,
This month which many reckon grey.
All too soon will summer come
With peonies scorching into bloom.

Then autumn's brittle leaves will fall
After the first wild winter squall;
And only the hoary oak will cling
To the last remnants of the spring.

Fiona – we must hope she'll be
As cunning as Penelope,
Stitches keep dropping every day:
Suitors and time best kept at bay.

A year or two, say five at least,
Before a grandchild's wedding feast;
And after that we'll hope to see
Replicas of all our three –
Yet none could be more sweet or fair
Than Angus, Jane and Susan Clare.

LOVE AND RAINBOWS

'Nothing changes,' she says,
'The Aga gurgles,
The kitchen smells of baked apples,
And all dogs look like Spruce.'

Perhaps she hasn't changed either,
Only this time it is *Das Kapital*
That lies open on the kitchen table.
She has bought sensible climbing boots.
'Five p. at a jumble sale,'
She explains.
Her grandfather is perplexed by the boots.
He has not seen silvered ones before.

'I needed this,' she says,
'To be alone on Loughrigg with my thoughts.'
Adding,
'Rainbows above the tumbling fells.'

Fiona wearing her great-great-great-aunt's dress and bonnet

FIONA

Fiona was born after we moved to Green Leas. Our doctor said she would not live. Constantly she lost weight. When she was weaned, someone gave us a present of caviare. It was the first time we had seen Fiona eat with relish. Caviare was not easily obtainable in wartime.

When she began to question, we became aware of her wisdom. 'Tell me,' she would begin; 'No, I'll tell you.' She would impart whatever it was with more insight than we could muster.

War makes unexpected impressions on a child's mind. She was convinced that Rudolph Hess had come down the hall chimney and was concealed somewhere in the house. From the nursery windows we watched the manoeuvres of Churchill tanks. 'Is Hitler too much even for God?' she wondered.

One day – she had just started school – she said, 'Mummy, you are a silly ass.' I was aghast. 'Fiona,' I gasped, 'If I had dared to say such a thing to my mother ...' Fiona looked at me appraisingly. 'But Granny never was one, was she?' she replied.

As parents, we were a disaster. Though we did try.

When I became eighty, I think I began to improve. The snag is that at any moment I may become a burden and the last ten years may be forgotten. To what do I attribute the improvement? Anne, mostly. Discovering the need to communicate.

Because of illness, Fiona had seldom more than one full week in any term. It was remarkable that she managed to acquire a diploma in Dairy Husbandry at Newton Rigg Farm Institute. She did this by writing the best farm diary of the year: that atoned for practically no marks for the measurement of a haystack.

She became Assistant Farm Manager at an Approved School. The girls loved and cherished her. No-one absconded when she took them to church or to visit another farm. She said it was a wonderful experience for one of the naughtiest girls (Fiona particularly chose her) to sit up all night with a sow that was farrowing.

Fiona and I shared an odd little bit of world that was exclusively ours. We all of us want someone who is completely our own. Oliver and I felt guilty because we had each other.

Fiona died in March 1980.

> You were my eyes, my ears, my touch,
> Does this surprise you now?
> They thought you were my shadow
> Those who did not know.

LEGACY

Snowdrops,
Hellebore,
Erica –
Brave flowers to bloom
When snow lies on the ground.
Another month
And her garden
Would have unfolded
Its carpet
Of purple at her feet.
Immune to cold,
Stooping, caressing,
Watching them open
Their petals to the sun,
The dark, the pale,
And those her favourites,
Slender and striped,
Dainty as children in their party clothes.
They, like Fiona,
Demanded no care.
So little to ask,
To know another spring
And see again
Her carpet of crocuses.

PELARGONIUM

She was convalescent when she bought
A geranium in a pot.
It did not flower.
After pruning it, watering it,
Carrying it from room to room
Following the sun,
Giving it Baby Bio,
It perked up but it did not flower.

A cactus sprang up as if from nowhere
And flourished in the shadow of the drooping geranium.

'If natural enemies of vipers –
Pigs, porcupines, hedgehogs,
Wild boars and turkeys – are not available,
An ordinary geranium in a pot keeps serpents at bay.'*
Therefore it appeared prudent to retain the geranium
In order to repel adders.

When she said, 'Today, distances seem less long,'
As though responding to an incantation,
The geranium produced buds: still more curious,
The cactus vanished.

Take care! While cherishing a geranium
You may be nurturing a cactus.
On the other hand, only if you suffer
From 'distances too long'
Will you appreciate perfection
In a pink pelargonium.

This really happened.

* Reported in 'The Times'

UNFINISHED PICTURE

She paints
A tree in mid air,
A bird table perched
Precariously
In emptiness.

I convert her nothingness
Into a waterfall.
Without the foundations she had laid
I could not build my folly.
Without her
My cataract
Would cease to flow.

She paints not as she sees
But her beliefs:
Feeling the chill of winter in the air
Her canvases consist of blasted trees
Devoid of bud or leaf,
Truth being bare.

SPRUCE
(Fiona's dog)

'Wa – alk!'
No scamper to the door,
Obedient as ever
But eyes pleading,
'Not too far.'

Following at heel
Until the bridge
Where she lay down,
Knowing Loughrigg
Loomed ahead,
Too steep for an old dog.

Cajoling, encouraging,
Somehow we reached the summit.
She sniffed the air
The old scents!
She couldn't believe it.

Years fell away,
Round and round she whirled;
A puppy again.
Oddly it made me cry.

She lay panting
At my feet,
The glory still alight
In her eyes.

'I'll take her home,'
I said,
'The way we came.'

'Please, please,'
Said the children,
'The path by the wood.'

Spruce knew, I knew,
The stile she could
No longer negotiate.

'We'll manage,
We'll get her over.'
Said the children.

Oh Spruce ...

If only ...

'The frail hair breadth
Of an if'

HAPPINESS

'I've given her everything; why can't she be happy?' Some are born happy, some acquire happiness, some apparently have it thrust upon them and don't take to it kindly.

It is odd that some babies are happy and some are not. Case Histories, that is what is required. Study the human concerned from birth to old age. Preferably arranging them in groups according to environment and family history. Is happiness due to pre-natal experience, health, genes, or just loving care? The ingredients must be love and loving; a sense of achievement; being needed, being useful.

Can we be happy when we are in pain? Pain of childbirth? Moments of intense happiness are shared moments.

Let me try and remember moments of happiness I've experienced alone. Lying in a hammock between an apple and a pear tree in blossom listening to the hum of bees. I was seven, I'd been ill and there were no lessons.

All my moments of childhood bliss have to do with gardens, the scent and feel of syringa, the taste of Victoria Plums, warm from the sun – they should have been left for Father, but two wouldn't be missed. So – that wasn't true happiness since it was partnered by guilt.

Happiness is a sense of communion with another person: sometimes interestingly with several people when life becomes a tapestry in the making (it was Muriel who supplied the word tapestry), when their lives become interwoven and each stitch is complementary to another.

> Don't go looking for it,
> It is as elusive
> As the foot of the rainbow:
> It comes unannounced:
> It is unpredictable,
> Inexplicable,
> Unforgettable:
> It is the moment
> When the tide turns
> And the world stands still.

TO ANNE IN ESSEX

If only you were here to share
This shadowy owl-light hour tonight,
To hear the blackbird's evening song
And see the lone rook's homing flight.

This spell of immortality
When Fairfield's smouldering flames ignite
Each crag to burn in Amaranth,
Jacinth, pearl, topaz, chrysolite.

Oak, ash, birch, pine and sycamore
They sway and murmur in the breeze,
Communicate in sylvan tongues –
Few understand the talk of trees.

Leave the balcony, shut the door
Cease my maundering, drop this pen –
At least I've shared my thoughts with you
As I'll share yours tonight at ten.

THE FIRST GREAT-GRANDCHILD

Hannah was born in Pietermaritzburg, South Africa, on 8th November 1987. Anne had gone out to be with Sue and Yunus. Oliver and I had promised not to die until after the birth and Anne was home again. Oliver was a very frail ninety-three-year-old by this time. He seemed to know when Sue was in labour; he always sensed when the family needed him.

CAROL FOR HANNAH 1987

Child of today, you travel far
On father's back, by plane and car
You take great wonders in your stride
That would make most eyes open wide;
Elephants no more bizarre
Than Herdwick sheep beneath Nab Scar.
A Protest March where banners sway
Resembling crowds in Bowness Bay.

This, your first Christmas, will it be
Akin to ours, with candled tree?
Does Africa grow trees like ours,
Will yours be decked with summer flowers?
Can every birth be harbinger
For peace, balm, frankincense and myrrh?
Infant of continent afar,
With you we share the Christmas Star.

Oliver had been in hospital for weeks early in 1987: he liked his fellow patients in the general ward and diagnosed their cases with Anne. He would have been happier with the Sisters and Nurses of long ago, who understood and loved him and would no doubt have done what he told them. Nevertheless, he marvelled at the skill of the young things who dealt so competently with the paraphernalia that surrounded him.

Now he was home in his own dressing room, the computer at his side; Anne was here. Knowing how ill he was she got up early on the last day of 1987 to see him. His bed was empty. She came through the open door to the next room and found us peacefully asleep together.

He died with his hand in mine. Anne and I had never known anyone could look so serene and beautiful.

Kenneth Cove, our former vicar came. 'I am here,' he began, 'because of a promise. What can I say of this remarkable man who, when he was being rushed to hospital, wrote a note in the ambulance – "I shall not be able to play the organ at Brathay tomorrow" – and furthermore persuaded the ambulance man to deliver the message to the vicarage.'

Oliver would have been amazed to know of the love and admiration he inspired even in his retirement.

Portrait of Oliver Lodge at Wraysholme

16TH JUNE 1988

When he was in the next room
I loved the house, its distances,
The standard roses he planted
Beneath the balcony where I could sit
'Sailing beyond the sunset,'
Waiting for the flitting of bats
And the first star.

Windows gleam, clean for the first time
In thirty years: fewer flexes
To trip over since being re-wired,
Yet a hermit's cell would seem more suitable
And all I ever wished if shared with O.
House! almost I hate you …

Not really, Fiona found you,
O. made music; it echoes still;

Neighbours observed him
Hoovering the roof
In an endeavour to eradicate
A nest of angry wasps,
Thereby disrupting
All TV sets in the area!
He still can make one laugh.

Each picture he painted
Communicates …
What is it they all say?
That something, quoting Ulysses,
'Some work … may still be done …'

Next week there will be Hannah, Anne and Sue –
The house still radiates his love.

GOODNIGHT, HOUSE

Will they turn you into flats,
Adding bathrooms here and there,
Convert cubby-holes to kitchens?

Craftsmen enjoyed the building of you,
Enjoyed the sensuous feel of seasoned pine,
Took pleasure in fitting every lock.

Owner, architect, builder,
With what care they chose
The Morris tiles; how foolishly
Planted the 'little' Redwood
Within walking distance of the door.

This summer evening
There's a presence on the balcony
Sharing the long shadows
And the flitting of the bats.

Will our ghosts haunt you,
Our music seep into your walls?
Will our robin escort you
From gate to door –
'Piping us aboard,' we call it.
Will jackdaws warn, scold, menace
According to their mood?

Meanwhile swifts have ceased their screaming,
Their acrobatic fantasies across a darkening sky:
Goodnight, House.

POSTSCRIPT: 1ST NOVEMBER 1992

All August she – the sycamore –
Watched balefully as I grew blind.
In this, the first November gale,
I can still see her branches sway,
Her falling leaves drift silently
Like tears upon an uncut lawn,
Yet maybe she is grateful for
The few that still remain. Next Spring
When daffodils surge round her roots
And children play, and lovers stroll
Beneath her shade I'll remember
I once saw her as a menace,
A single eye – a slit in her
Thick foliage – appeared a threat.
The oak, the ash, the thorn were trees –
She seemed a witch casting a spell,
Weaving a shroud of deepest black
Where no sun shone, nor moon, nor stars.

──────── Chapter Ten ────────

FULL CIRCLE

Jane asked if I was glad to have had these last three years. Years without Oliver. I can't get *Pilgrim's Progress* out of my head. It's all there. The Slough of Despond, Giant Despair, the Valley of the Shadow. Christiana's journey was smoother than Christian's. The Happy Ending was when everyone got safely across the River. The Land of Beulah was where they waited for the crossing.

Can I answer Jane's question? I don't know, so I'll stop writing. What I do know is that nothing can take away what you have had.

SWAN FEATHER

Preening his plumage, swan loosens a feather.
Pinion's mains'l the light breezes fill
Floating down river in halcyon weather,
All summer captive to one snowy quill.
Gaily eluding the hand of piscator,
Rock in the river diverting its course,
Free to sail downstream without any charter,
Galleon steered by invincible force.
Where are you bound for with your precious cargo
Lashed in the hold of your wild white swan quill?
Memory's havens impose no embargo –
These you may enter and anchor at will.

Oliver was fishing the Eamont when this occurred. He saw the feather floating towards him and remembered his grandfather cutting a quill pen. What is more, he had recently annexed a penknife which had been my father's. It had two blades: at the hinge of one there was a contrivance resembling a cigar cutter for shaping the quill; the other blade was razor sharp for trimming and slitting the point. He had an urge to develop the skill himself. He leaned forward to grasp the feather and fell headlong into the pool.

This poem becomes poignant as banks become unaccountably steep, stones slippery and waders begin to take in water. At the time,

Sheona with her grandmother

I thought it silly and sentimental. However, Roger Fiske set it to music, I imagine because he could see in his mind the feather twisting and twirling and hear the ripple of water.

The Swan Feather picks up its load at any old port, dumps it at 'the haven' and sails with the current, which takes me back to my childhood. A walled garden with hollyhocks. A piece of Harrogate toffee if I drank all my milk.

A walk with Granny: she wore a black silk dress that trailed on the ground, a black mantle, a black bonnet with a white frill inside and broad white ribbons that tied underneath her chin. Her gloves were grey. Her umbrella had a silver handle. There were no flowers in the lane, only gorse. I desperately wanted a flower and gorse was prickly. Granny picked a piece for me. 'I'll carry it,' she said. 'We'll put it in water when we get home.' She pretended not to notice the spots of blood on her glove ...

When Mother and Father went to Scotland, I stayed with Granny and Aunt Gus. After lunch each day, Aunt Gus went to lie down in her room and I went with Granny to her sofa under the window. She read *Black Beauty* to me. 'If it makes you cry, should we not find another book?' she said. 'No, no, go on. Please go on,' I pleaded.

Granny was deaf. 'I love that child,' she said once, as I was leaving her room, not knowing she was thinking aloud.

She had a green parrot. It flew free and was chased by crows.

In the room known as the North Pole, there were photographs of her eleven children. They were all hale and hearty and very good-looking. Jane Jobling and an under-nurse looked after them. When they were young, they trooped into Granny's bedroom to say good morning to her. She always had breakfast in bed.

Granny went to school in Edinburgh. In a handsome edition of *Poems and Plays of Oliver Goldsmith*, the inscription on the fly leaf says, 'Four Royal Circus, Senior English Prize'. Granny preferred Sir Walter Scott.

Thoughts are too elusive to be captured in chronological order. Try writing NORTHALLERTON – see what happens.

Mary Harrison coming to take me for a walk in my push chair. Her favourite walk was through the Applegarth that ended in a narrow path beneath the Vicarage wall. Instead of turning right and going home through the town, we went in the other direction and came to big iron gates leading to a strange place.

Mother had told me that Fairy Stories weren't really true but I wondered if she was mistaken because this must be the garden of the Snow Queen. Stretching in more or less straight lines were shiny white slabs of stone – perhaps they were icicles. Flowers didn't grow – they lay, some fresh, others faded, on the ground. Yet it also had something to do with Heaven, which was as puzzling as the story of Kay and Gerda. Mary did not explain and I had an idea that this was not the walk that Mother had intended.

Later came lessons at The Close, Brompton. The Royal children's sailor suits were made from Brompton linen; so were our towels. On the way to Osmotherly, fields were white with linen bleaching in the sun. Brompton had a stream and a village green. The mill was not in sight; one just knew it was there.

The Close was on the top of the hill above the village and, unlike any other house, it wasn't old. It had a front courtyard and a back one where the stables were and where Greta kept her white rats. The Yeomans who owned the Mill lived there. There were Mr. and Mrs. Yeoman and Greta and Joyce, who were clever and would some time be going away to school. Kathleen too would be going away in due course. Betty was younger than the others and it was imagined that she needed a companion of her own age. I expect I was the only one available. In fact, it was Kathleen who was my friend. They had long hair and Nana brushed it till it shone more than anyone else's hair. She tried to brush out my curls, but they would come back.

It was too far to walk to Brompton and Father needed the car, so every morning, Close (he was the groom and it was odd that he should also be called Close) came for Miss Guthrie and for me in the Governess Cart. Close said, 'Good morning, Little Miss White Riding Hood,' because I wore my white serge cape and hood.

I didn't like lessons but I loved the house. The wide shallow staircase, the corridors, the bathrooms, the large hall with its inglenook. The schoolroom had proper desks and windows looking over the terrace, the croquet lawn and the shrubbery in the distance.

Miss Guthrie said, 'If a herring and a half costs three ha'pence, how much would two cost?' 'First the sprats, then the herrings and after that, the whales,' said the Loch Fyne fishermen. I knew about herrings but I couldn't imagine a half one. Was it alive or dead?

I cried and Miss Guthrie was cross and after that we concentrated on writing pot hooks. Everyone imagined that I could read, but I couldn't. I just knew *Peter Rabbit* by heart and knew when to turn each page. 'The cat sat on the mat' was a revelation. I owe Miss Guthrie that. The one total joy of lessons was listening to Greta and Joyce reciting 'The Forsaken Merman'.

Sheona with (unsacrificed) doll

At eleven o'clock we adjourned to the nursery where Nana resided. There were grapes and peaches from the greenhouse and milk from the Jersey herd. After that, we played 'Hare and Hounds' in the garden and Miss Guthrie became really nice.

One day at dancing class, I saw Mother take Betty on her knee and wrap her in her fur-lined coat. Betty died the next day. Edward VII hadn't yet had the first operation for appendicitis.

Now I became really and truly Kathleen's friend. We played 'Trappers and Indians'. Greta and Joyce had a curious game called 'Human Sacrifices'. This was played in the shrubbery and Kathleen and I were not allowed to participate. We watched from behind a tree. It simply meant lighting a fire and burning an old doll on a flat stone.

Beyond the shrubbery was Vardy's cottage. He and his four sons were gardeners and Vardy would not have approved of a bonfire and that was what made the game somewhat risky. A barn owl lived in the building next to Vardy's cottage.

Their uncle, Dr. Yeoman, was one of the partners in Father's practice and was only a doctor because he wanted to do something useful. He and Dr. Hutchinson went to France for their holidays. Ours were fishing ones in Aberdeenshire and Argyll. Father, I think, did all the surgery at the Cottage Hospital that had the second oldest vine in England over the doorway, a long narrow garden with a tennis court, panelled rooms, Chippendale chairs and bright fires.

'Granny with the Curls' (in fact they were ringlets) and her daughter Miss Jane Yeoman lived near us with Darius the cat, a companion and two maids. In 1924, when we went to Switzerland, Miss Jane gave me a real hoop to wear under Oliver's grandmother's skirt for a fancy dress dance, and her father's wedding trousers for Oliver.

Mrs. Harry Yeoman lived in the house facing the Brompton village green. Her parties were especially good. She played the piano for 'Oranges and Lemons' and 'Nuts in May'. Choices. At what an early age they begin and never cease. As it grew dark, we danced 'Sir Roger de Coverley'. The garden beyond the French windows became mysterious.

There were Osmotherley Yeomans too. They had a governess who wrote books for children. A daughter travelled on the Trans-Siberian Train and wrote a novel that became a film which still turns up on television today. I wish she could have known this would happen.

Robert Louis Stevenson's nephew came to parties at The Close. Mrs. Yeoman died, which was very sad. Later, Kathleen left her school and came to mine, Skellfield, so we were always friends.

Greta and Joyce became doctors. When I married Oliver and he operated at the Rutson Hospital, Joyce said did I know why he liked her to give anaesthetics and I said no. She laughed and said, 'Because he likes to give his own.'

THEIR SINGINGS AND THEIR GIFTS

A flock of geese, driven like sheep through the town,
Their cackling anxious, forlorn, unlike the cry,
Eerie and magical, of wild geese.
Where had they come from?
Where were they going?

* * *

Awakened by Father, carried in his arms
To the front door to listen to curlew,
Redshank, sandpipers, flying to their inland nesting site:
An unseen legion, calling, signalling to one another.

* * *

A bear in chains, dancing just for Father and for me
In a lane blue with cranesbill and butterflies.
His keepers were Russian, said Father, and gave them half a crown.

* * *

German bands. 'Spies, all of them,' said Father.

* * *

Votes for Women: Father approved.
I never asked Mother.

'In the spring a livelier iris changes on the burnish'd dove.' There was a dovecote in the garden. Father carried me up a ladder to look into the eyes of Blue Nun pigeons, presumably to see if their irises were lively. Father said that of all the poets Tennyson was the most observant of little details like this.

Later, in *Locksley Hall*, Tennyson talks about airy navies raining ghastly dew. I don't think Father ever visualised this. He thought aeroplanes would never be safe. The first one we saw crashed in the field of the agricultural show, and we watched three race across England. It was a very hot day, someone gave me ginger ale to drink and I felt sick.

Those were the days of German bands. 'Spies, every one of them,' said Father. In August, probably 1910 or 1911, there was a German waiter at the Argyll Arms, a good looking young man. Eighty years on we would have imagined he was a student working in the vacation. In 1911 Father knew that he was a spy. I was amazed to hear Father consulting a waiter about fishing, especially about fishing in Loch Fyne. We only fished the Shira and, when invited, the Castle water.

At breakfast, 'I want to spear flat fish,' said Father, 'They inhabit very deep water I believe.' (Deep enough to harbour the German Navy?) 'What do you imagine the depth to be … ?' He mentioned some particular place. The waiter replied without hesitation. 'About … ' I can't remember the number of fathoms but it was proof enough for my father. The waiter must not guess the motive of the interrogation.

That very day we set off in a rowing boat. Mother was not enthusiastic about the expedition; after an hour or so we landed her on a tiny island. She was reading happily when she heard an extraordinary sound – 'A bull' she thought. She was terrified of bulls, but how could a bull arrive on an island in the middle of the loch? Looking down she saw an immense whale in the process of stranding itself almost at her feet. It had been her own choice to land on that island but now she was exceedingly cross with us for leaving her alone in an expanse of loch with no land or help in sight. Father and I were away for a long time. I can't remember if we speared any flat fish.

A few nights later Germans from a very fine yacht came into the hotel and we saw one of them pop a note into the box that stood in the hall: a box that was emptied by our waiter ...

In August 1914 Father was Doctor and Commandant of a Red Cross Hospital. He did not live to see 'airy navies raining ghastly dew'. Sometimes I wonder what he would have thought of television. 'Tennyson foresaw that too when he wrote *The Lady of Shalott*,' he might have said. Apart from news and nature films I think ·he would have regarded TV as a 'fritterer away of time'.

In those days death seemed so tragic, yet my parents accepted theirs and with serenity, each in their turn thinking of others rather than themselves. 'Remember the Little Trout,' said my Father, as I kissed him goodbye. Fiona was born three months later.

SAYINGS OF FATHER AND SPOTS OF TIME

'Drive through any village,' said Father, 'and you can tell if it has a good Schoolmaster and a good Vicar.' 'We owe a lot to the great landowners,' he continued. 'It is they who made the countryside beautiful.'

'"I come from haunts of coot and hern,"' quoted Father, as we crossed the field to the willow, where our fishing began. 'Do you know what a "hern" is?' I don't believe I even bothered to guess because I knew he would tell me.

The Beck overgrown, dark and secret, but when a sudden breeze ruffled the leaves, the sun shone through and dappled the water. 'That is what Tennyson meant,' explained Father, 'when he said, "See the netted sunbeams dance."' We were as much a part of the Beck as the kingfisher, dipper, heron and otter.

A walk with Father was as rare and memorable as a bicycle ride with Mother. On the hillside near Mount Grace, we came across a rabbit in a snare. Father released it gently. It seemed not to be badly injured. 'I hope,' said Father, 'that the man's children won't go hungry tonight. His wife is probably relying on the rabbit for their supper.'

NO PROOF

Dear Computer,

You remind me of the legend of 'The Man of Richmond' who, one late afternoon when he was sauntering round the wall of the castle, noticed the outline of an archway etched in the rough stone: maybe it was a trick of light, a shaft from the setting sun. He traced it with his finger and to his amazement, a door rolled open. He could see nothing. He dared not take a step forward in to dark, indefinite space. He remembered he had a box of matches in his pocket. There were two left. He struck one. Before him was a great hall; in its centre, a round table. He thought he could discern figures. The match went out. He lit the other and indeed there were figures: figures of men in armour and they appeared to be asleep. The match burned his finger. As he let it fall, the door swung back and he stood gazing at a blank wall.

He marked the place and ran to tell his family, who did not believe one word of his story. 'Come and see,' he urged them, and reluctantly they agreed. On the way others, hearing the story, joined the group and so there was a crowd watching as he ran his hand over the wall where he knew the door to be – if only he could find the spring. The on-lookers dispersed. They'd never believed him anyway. He had no proof …

No proof. That, dear computer, is what reminded me of the legend. Yesterday I wrote a story on your screen. Today, the screen is blank.

CYCLING

Mother was a cycling pioneer. She had lessons from a very good man. In her day, neat ankles were an asset and one of the few opportunities a girl had of displaying them was when mounting a bicycle – an inch allowed, no more.

When I acquired a bicycle, she tried to impart the art to me: heels down, head up, back straight. She rode effortlessly, majestically.

One memorable day, we went blackberrying together. We were invited by the wife of a farmer who said that, after we had gathered as many as we liked, she would give us tea. Tea in the farmhouse kitchen smelling of newly baked bread and with a long deal table in front of the windows, spread with scones, buns, cheesecakes, maids of honour, freshly churned butter and cream. Eight miles there and eight miles back through country lanes, Mother all to myself.

Mother loved jigsaws. There were boxes of them in the bottom drawer of her bureau. The mind becomes rather like that drawer; individual boxes long since disintegrated, the pieces lying in confusion, yet a word or question can bring to the surface one segment, its shape and colour providing the key to the picture.

JIGSAW: MISSING PIECES

Time's clock
Ticks dispassionately on:
Despite disorder
Pieces fall
Into their destined place:
A picture emerges
The subject still obscure,
I see a river,
I see the children,

I see the setting sun
Stroking winter bracken:

Maybe this jigsaw
Cannot be completed
In one lifetime.

NOW AND THEN

Nothing changed. White violets – Father knew where they grew hidden under damp leaves. Then the lane blue with cranesbill and butterflies, next came roses, meadowsweet and Queen Anne's lace. Masses of butterflies, orange tips, red admirals, tortoiseshells and meadow browns. Fields full of haycocks. In the garden syringa, black cherries out of reach, plums and apricots ripening on the wall, and raspberries behind the summer house. In the greenhouse a frog, a caterpillar which became a chrysalis and later, while Father and I were watching, turned into a privet hawk moth. We opened the door and he flew away. There were grapes too, small but sweet.

Sounds seem to be hum of bees and church bells. The curfew rang every night at eight. Horses' hooves at six in the morning and six in the evening when Mr. Finkle brought the milk. Sometimes honking of geese, not flying overhead, but driven through the town in a flock like sheep. They paused sometimes to nibble grass which grew by the roadside. The most mysterious noise was when it was dusk and cloud after cloud of curlew, red shank and sandpipers flew inland to nest. You couldn't see them but they felt so close you imagined you could hear the beat of their wings. Their pipings seemed not of this world.

Once a year in the distance was the music of merry-go-rounds. Father took me to the north end of the town. There were stalls lit by flares. I longed to ride on one of the horses, but Father wouldn't hear of that.

It was the only time I ever walked through the town with him. Sometimes I went shopping with Mother, Russell's – the grocer – smelled of coffee. Miss Attlee's – where we bought French buns – of newly baked bread. We made our own. You could smell leather long before you reached the saddlers. Smithson's the stationers was the most interesting shop, because it was there you bought your penny dolls for the dolls' house. Mother dressed them. There was a cook, a parlour-maid, a chauffeur and the Master and Mistress. They couldn't be children because the dolls were all the same size. Their faces were different, or so we thought, black dots for eyes, nose and mouth. They had to be carefully chosen for the toy theatre.

Miss Peacock sold reels of cotton and silk for embroidery. It was interesting because her brother owned racing stables. Incidentally Mr. Smithson was interesting too because he was distantly related to the Duke of Northumberland.

There was another fascinating shop north of the Surgery House and the Golden Lion. Upstairs there were beautiful jugs and basins and mugs with a frog at the bottom. You drank your milk in order to see its head gradually appear. You only shopped when there was something you needed such as candles or bacon or oranges. It was only if you took a train to Harrogate that you bought something as a treat. A bed for the dolls' house or a tiny bronze animal. You only went to Harrogate once a year. Stations, even large ones like Newcastle, were calm and unhurried. There was a waiting room at the Station with a fire, a round table and a motherly person who remembered one and dusted the chairs and made everything look bright and cheerful. Stations were nice places. Ticket collectors smiled and addressed one as 'hinny', friendly porters found one a seat next to the window facing the engine. The disadvantages of trains in those days were that there were no corridors and sometimes the journey was long. On the other hand there were luncheon baskets with cold chicken, rolls and butter and lettuce. Also foot warmers. If one was lucky racing pigeons were being released from their baskets. They flew round for a few minutes before setting out in the right direction. Our green parrot liked the station. We were told that he perched on the roof but he always came home.

One reason that made life seem secure when I was little was the unalterableness of time. I remember every detail about what we had for breakfast in 1904, even the patterns on the damask tablecloth. Breakfast at nine. At Father's end of the table a green coffee pot, a heavy silver-plated bacon dish, heavy because it was filled with boiling water, and a silver toast rack. Father's breakfast was porridge (best medium Midlothian oatmeal that Mother ordered from Edinburgh), toast and marmalade. And the *Yorkshire Post*.

Mother sat at the other end of the table with *The Times*, a silver teapot, jug and sugar basin. She had cream and I always hoped for a little on my porridge. I had treacle (the golden sort) on mine until I was eight and knew better. A triangular contraption supported four egg cups but only one egg. When there were visitors there was cold ham on the sideboard, that they could carve for themselves. Luncheon at one.

Maybe a privileged world but not a wealthy one. Father was a physician and surgeon probably with no private means. We had two maids, a chauffeur – he was a necessity. There were gates to open, lots of punctures, traps to be led past because it was a country practice and horses weren't used to cars. Oh! and Mrs Ward who came on Mondays to light the boiler and wash the clothes. On Tuesdays she ironed with a flat iron heated on the kitchen range. She spat on them to see if they were ready to use.

There was snow in winter. Father drove a horse-drawn sledge. He had one of the first cars in the county. Its number was A.J.8. Father won an electric brougham in a competition. It was not good as a country car so he exchanged it for two others which is why we had three cars. Looking back it seems an absurd extravagance for a not-well-off country doctor. He was mad about cars and invented a carburetter but it didn't occur to him to have it patented. His friend was a friend of Rolls.

In those early days there was a chauffeur called Radcliffe who looked as grand as my dolls' house one. We ended up years later with a boy who cleaned the car and carried the coals and didn't wear uniform. (That reminds me that Oliver's father had a 'boy in buttons' to answer the door to patients.) Mother went to a garden party in the car and it broke down before it got to the drive and all the people in carriages bowed politely but Mother knew they were smiling to them-

The three cars near Northallerton

selves. Now they say you can't find a place to park the car in North-allerton – then the cobbled curbs were empty.

'People' were Town or Country, Church or Chapel, Conservative or Liberal. This is probably why I say now as I watch television, 'Won't Heaven be lovely; no money, no politics, no motorways.'

I suspect – it never occurred to me then – that Father may some-times have been anxious about money. I didn't like it when instead of telling me the story of Eyes and No Eyes, he talked about Tariff Reform and Free Trade. I didn't know which was good or what was bad, but one was much better for farmers. The dangerous road where accidents occurred – Father was Surgeon as well as Physician – was the Leeming Lane that was straight and narrow compared with our twisting, gated roads, and there cars probably exceeded the twenty-eight-miles-an-hour speed limit.

People were probably no happier in the days before the 1914–18 war, when 'England ruled the waves thereby ensuring Freedom of the Seas for everyone, bringing justice to all corners of the Earth, enjoying the best Civil Service, Police Force and the purest water', than they are now, but they were certainly less confused because there appeared to be two sides to most questions instead of twenty. Perhaps it is TV that has changed the world: new ideas batter us like hailstones. My Father said that when he was a house surgeon in Newcastle Infirmary in 1884 the local newspaper reported that a man had committed suicide with phosphorus poison (sucking matches?). Father had never seen such a case before, but several more came in quick succession. He wrote to the papers describing the painful effects of phosphorus poison and no more came.

When I watch violence on TV I remember this. Yes, that is the difference. We were certain in the years before 1912 that the world was growing better. Soon there would be better education for everyone, no poverty. We ask ourselves now is man any less cruel that he was in pre-history? Scientists always questioned but today the 'man in the street' questions too. Man contemplates germ warfare and finds means of bringing back cholera and black death; on the other hand he is hopeful of finding means to cure cancer. Meanwhile the world is overcrowded. What can he do about that?

The final question is Death. Odd, isn't it, that that is a door that has not been opened. What do we – the old – think about it? The process of dying we all fear, the 'being a burden, dependent on others, pain'. Death itself is interesting. If the door opens we'll know and understand (hopefully!) the things that puzzle us.

YOU

You
In your wisdom
Conceived
The evolution
Of caddis to dragonfly;
The life style
Of the river fluke.

You
Gave the flycatcher
Courage
And tenacity.

You
Having endowed
The last
Of your imaginings
With the capacity
To think;

Can you,
In all fairness,
Ask him
To believe?

If only You had not said,
'Let Us make Man in Our image.'

It's no good:
It's impossible to end there,
There is need –
Galaxies and aeons of it –
To believe.
A filament to which to cling,
Fragile
As a spider's thread
Which you'd think
Might be swept away by
Scientist's brush,
Or duster of the humanist:
As far as the unknown is concerned
How can even they be
Infallible?

STANG

When I became too old for walks in a pram and too young for lessons,
I went with Father on his rounds. At ten o'clock, I sat in the hall next
to the grandfather clock in my white cape and hood, buttoned boots
and gaiters, with Leo, my pekinese, at my feet; Lord Roberts, the cat,
at his side; and the guinea pigs in a basket. Companions were re-
quired because 'visits' were sometimes long. I also had a mouth organ
that I couldn't play.

The car was the red Argyll with shining brass lamps. Radcliffe sat
at the back to open gates, lead horses past when they were fright-
ened, and mend punctures.

Father put his Eyes and No Eyes stories into practice. I became the
good little girl who knew if a flower belonged to the order Legumi-
nosae, Cruciferae or Umbelliferae. I couldn't read but I could spell
ESCHSCHOLTZIA because his mother had taught him to spell that

An outing by car, the red Argyll with shining brass lamps

Mother with Sheona and Mr. Rutson

when he was my age and anyway they grew in the garden. He suggested that I should call the guinea pigs Alpha, Beta, Gamma and Delta: I didn't know why. Alpha was the father guinea pig but Delta was the nicest of the four, so when there were babies, I gave them to her in a separate hutch. She ate them.

Sometimes Father took me into the surgery to watch him make up medicines. It was like a room in Beatrix Potter's *The Pie and the Patty Pan*. Father's medicines cured coughs and rheumatism in a miraculous way. He said the secret was always to buy the best ingredients. He and Mother said about everything that it was cheaper in the long run to buy the best.

Some visits were better than others. There was the farm where I was allowed to go into the orchard and pick as many snowdrops as I liked; Watergate, where something exciting was always happening in the kitchen – a lamb in front of the fire or goslings on the table being fed. 'Difficult creatures to rear.' There were calves too, and baby pigs.

Then there was Newby Hall. Mr. Rutson was blind. Every spring I was summoned to take him round the garden, which was in fact a park, to talk about the flowers which he seemed to see as well as I did, never forgetting their names. It was sad one year when we came to the lake because the mallard were without feet. A pike had nipped them off. Mr. Rutson gave me a golden sovereign.

Perhaps all children know when their parents are sad or anxious and remember events that are never told. When we drove through the village of Romanby, we passed a house with a walled garden at the far end of the village green. I knew that here something had happened that concerned Father. The house was empty, the occupants had been frightened and had fled.

Years later, a story filtered through to me. Men had gathered in the North End with torches in their hands, four of them carrying the effigy of a man on a pole, or 'stang'. They marched, chanting a sinister 'Ran tan tan' to the rattle of tin cans. The crowd arrived to find the house empty. Father had warned the victim. I have the impression that the man was both a patient and a friend of Father's. It was a case of a 'wronged' girl and Father had sympathy for her and her parents. Because of the respect folk had for him, he had been able to prevent a horrifying event. The Riding of the Stang never occurred again. There is no-one left to vouch for the accuracy of this account. What a story Hardy could have made of it.

Among the jigsaw pieces, I find this letter from Mrs. Gott about my father: 'He belonged to the generation when the country practitioner was far more than Doctor to the body. He became the intimate and loved friend of all ... never a week passed without meeting and learning something of bird, insect or flower from him.'

CURATES

Curates conscientiously called on parishioners on foot and in all weathers. Busy farmers and their wives sometimes found this inconvenient.

One wild blustery afternoon, Mr. Armstrong chose to call on a farm some distance away. The farmer's wife gave him tea. He seemed so happy sitting in front of the kitchen fire that, a few hours later, she was compelled to ask him to stay for supper. Mr. Armstrong accepted with delight. The husband endeavoured to conceal his irritation and impatience. She could hear the rain battering against the windows. 'How can I turn him out?' she wondered and in desperation suggested that he should stay the night. She could not understand why Mr. Armstrong should appear to be so embarrassed. He stuttered, he turned red: he seemed unable to reply ...

'I shall have to go and lock up the animals,' she told him and went away to confer with her husband. Reluctantly he agreed to harness the trap and take the man home. There seemed to be no alternative. They returned to the kitchen and Mr. Armstrong had gone. No thanks, no message. They went to bed.

About two in the morning, they were awakened by a thumping on the front door. The farmer flung open the window and hurled abuse at the wet shrunken little figure he supposed to be a tramp standing below. A voice replied, 'I have been home for my pyjamas ...'

MR. DUCKWORTH

The first Northallerton church was built by Paulinus in the year 1162. It was destroyed in 1318 when the Scots sacked the town and rebuilt again between 1345 and 1381. In 1847 the pews, though in excellent state, were taken down and replaced by stalls or free sittings.

Mother had a model of the church. It was Anne's favourite plaything. The stalls were the right size for her horses and cows. Anne is still convinced that it was the duck in the pulpit that horrified the curate, Mr. Duckworth, and made him carry off her beloved farm.

Forty years later, fate led her to the church and there was her 'farm' in a glass case and a note saying that the history of this valuable work was unknown and that it had been restored to the church by the wife of some Canon. Now, children are not allowed to touch the model. No hens and cockerels roost above the nave. Its pews and pulpit are empty. It is sixty years on and Anne is still a bit resentful.

BAZAAR

1907 was the year that *Tales of Troy and Greece* by Andrew Lang was published. It was also the year of the Church Bazaar.

Mother and I went to tea at the Vicarage. Mona, Tommy and I played in the nursery. Mona, who was eight and clever, told us about Titania and her fairies. As we were leaving, the Vicar said there were to be Tableaux Vivants at the Bazaar and I was to be a fairy in *A Midsummer Night's Dream*. Mother made the fairy dress and it was beautiful – white gauze dotted with pearls.

Each morning, we went to the Town Hall to rehearse. On the platform, there was a mossy bank that was really benches covered in scratchy green baize. Titania's fairies had names like Peaseblossom and Mustardseed, and Tommy, the only boy, was Puck. We sat very still until the curtain came down and then the Vicar rearranged us, and that was a Tableau Vivant.

On the day of the Bazaar, the stalls looked lovely. They had red and white canopies and there was a Bran Tub. Whenever I saw Mother, I asked her for pennies for the Bran Tub. It was full of parcels wrapped in paper so you didn't know what was inside; it was very exciting.

Someone gave me a picture to carry. I didn't know why. It was called a 'raffle'. It was quite small and had a gold frame. It was a watercolour of Richmond Castle painted by the Hon. Mrs. Hutton. Ladies in large hats said to me, 'What is your name, dear?', wrote it down on a little white card which they dropped in a box.

Then came the Tableau Vivant. Instead of Mona, I sat on the top of the Mound. Afterwards we stood on the platform and the Vicar gave me a book and said, 'Now we will sing "God Save the King."' 'I don't know the words,' I said. 'Never mind,' he said quite crossly, 'just sing.'

Eighty-four years on I ask, what is the story behind my childish memory of the Church Bazaar and who should be Titania? Mother and the Vicar's wife were equally determined. 'To put it to the vote' seems a drastic way of solving a trivial problem. The Vicar must have been at his wit's end.

I still have the edition of *Tales of Troy and Greece*.

THE SQUIRREL

'If I had a squirrel,' thought the child, 'I should be happy; perhaps someone will give me one for Christmas.' Christmas came and Christmas went. 'If I had a squirrel,' said the child, 'a real squirrel to sit on my shoulder and eat out of my hand, I should be good.'

One day, there was a party. It was a special party because it was so far away, at the other side of the county. 'I shall wear my brooch,' said the child. The brooch belonged to Mother when she was a little girl; it was a swallow made of pearls and it had a tiny gold heart hanging from its beak. Mother was taking the child to the party. It was a long drive and the house, when they got there, was in the middle of a forest. The child went upstairs to take off her hat and her coat. There were other children, but she did not know them: they looked at her and she looked at them, but they did not speak to her, though they talked to one another.

The party was in a very big room and in the middle of the room there was a tree. Not the sort of Christmas tree with coloured lights you have at home, but a tall forest tree. On the branches hung presents and on the top-most twig, there was a squirrel. It was exactly like a real squirrel: it had a bushy tail; it was the kind of squirrel you hug and take to bed with you. The child saw nothing else. She gazed at the tree and at the squirrel sitting there, looking so real. A piano was being played and someone cried, 'Musical chairs!' and seized the child's hand. After that there were more games and then tea. It was a pity to leave the tree, but in the dining room there was a long table and a cake with seven candles. Someone had to help the girl whose birthday it was to cut the cake, and everyone helped to blow out the candles. There were half oranges filled with jelly and a cake like a log of wood made of chocolate.

Tea was over and they moved to another, smaller, room where there was a conjuror. The boys laughed and clapped and rushed forward to help the conjuror when he said, 'Who will hold this card for me?' or 'Who will lend me a watch?' The child was only interested in the two white rabbits which the conjuror produced from out of his hat.

They went back to the big room. 'Put out the lights,' they cried, and when this was done, the glow from the candles enveloped the tree in a misty radiance. All you could see of the squirrel was a faint shadow. 'They are going to give the presents,' whispered someone and the children surged forward. One girl – she was quite old, nearly nine perhaps, with long hair falling over her shoulders – pushed to the front, crying 'Aunty, Aunty, may I have the squirrel?' 'Yes dear,' said the hostess, 'Bring a step ladder, someone.' A step ladder was brought, the squirrel was handed down to the girl with the shining hair, who clutched it to her and danced away. 'Has everyone got a present?' The child moved slowly forward to receive the only one that was left – a chocolate doll in a gilt bed. 'Thank you very much,' she said. A few minutes later she was in the hall, saying 'Thank you for a lovely party.' The girl with the long hair was there with the squirrel in her arms.

Outside the air crackled with frost, the trees near the house shone in the light streaming from the windows and from the open door. Above, the sky was ablaze with stars. 'If I lived in the forest,' thought the child, 'one day I should go for a walk all alone and find a baby squirrel caught in a trap. It would be cold and hungry and frightened. I would bring it home with me and make it better. If I lived in the forest,' she mused, 'and had a squirrel, I should be happy.'

HAIKU

Until the tide turns,
Limpets, unaware of time,
Dream their lives away.

At the edge of time
Waiting for the tide to turn.
Will the sea be calm?

ICEBERG VOICES

Deaf to the conversation
Of whales and dolphins,
To the moans of your sisters
As they calve in the abyss.
Unable to interpret
The intuition of salmon
On their journey in mid-Atlantic,
All the deaf noise of sounds
That never cease.

Sheona with her granddaughter Jane

Four generations at Wraysholme

I should like to say more about Jane and Tibet, but the sun shines on the computer screen and I can't see.

The grandchildren have led a more adventurous life than mine, and have seen more of the world: they are more courageous than I am – instead of trying to escape from violence and pain, they combat it. They work terribly hard but they do have fun. One of the good things about becoming old is that it brings one closer to one's family.

Last night I went with Josefina and Muriel to Molly Lefebure's lecture on Coleridge's Great Walk, illustrated by slides and music. It made me ask: is this what Jane sometimes felt in Tibet? Angus had an inkling of it on Mount Sinai; Sue, when she stood on the border summit between Iran and India as the sun rose. Mountains terrifying, magnificent, occasionally lovely and gentle, making one think of Genesis, the beginning of the world. What had inspired such photographs by Molly's husband, John Gerrish? What made Molly choose Ravel's *Daphnis and Chloë* to interpret them? The answer can only be found outside words, as I tried to say in my 'Ode to O'.

Jane asked me about this sonnet at the beginning of this book. Why 'baths' of 'all the western stars'? Another question impossible to answer, but Oliver and I knew exactly what Tennyson meant as we sailed into that sunset. And that is still true.

FULL CIRCLE

Catapulted
Into a chilly
Hostile world
From warmth and safety.

Maybe the exit
Will be less traumatic
Than the entrance:
Integration this time,
No severance.

Sheona, 1993
(Photo: Paul Renouf)